JUST JUGGLE

JUST JUGGLE

Steve Cohen

Illustrations
by Frank Weiss

McGRAW-HILL BOOK COMPANY

New York St. Louis San Francisco Auckland Bogotá
Guatemala Hamburg Johannesburg Lisbon London
Madrid Mexico Montreal New Delhi Panama Paris
San Juan São Paulo Singapore Sydney Tokyo Toronto

Copyright © 1982 by Steve Cohen

1 2 3 4 5 6 7 8 9 0 FGRFGR 8 7 6 5 4 3 2

ISBN 0-07-011623-7

LIBRARY OF CONGRESS CATALOGING IN PUBLICATION DATA

Cohen, Steve, 1950–
  Just juggle
  1. Jugglers and juggling. I. Title.
GV1547.C59 1982   793.8   82-9885
ISBN 0-07-011623-7   AACR2

BOOK DESIGN: JUDY ALLAN

For Sean, who laughs when I juggle

Acknowledgments

As a book gestates, a writer incurs debts that may be difficult to repay. Friends, family members, and strangers offer encouragement, express interest, provide support in ways large and small. My gratitude reaches back to everyone who assisted in the birth of this volume. Many thanks to:

Carol Weimann, Lake Tahoe, California, for teaching me how to juggle.

Frank Weiss, our artist.

Howard Suss, of New York City, for shooting the film that became the flipbook and the stills that became illustrations, as well as for his good spirits and giving fellowship that always set standards of friendship.

Jay Siegel, research photographer.

Curtis W. Casewit, of Denver, Colorado, for teaching me how to juggle being a writer.

Rich Chamberlin, of Kenmore, New York, and Gene Jones, of New York City, officers of The International Juggler's Association, for their generous technical help.

Debbie Martin, of Hollywood, Florida, ace typist.

Larry Goodman, of North Miami, Florida, my favorite juggling partner.

The many people at McGraw-Hill, whose time and efforts have made this book possible. I regret that I cannot name them all. Hearty thanks to Bob Mitchell, Art Director, for his eagle eyes, and PJ Haduch, Assistant Editor, for breaking the ice. And extra special thanks to Joanne Dolinar, Senior Editor, for expert and top-notch care in every respect.

And to Jodie, my wife, confidante and sounding board, for bearing with me while I wrote this book.

—S.C.
July, 1982

Contents

PART III: The Method

PART IV: Continuity

PART
I

Introduction

THE PURPOSE OF THIS BOOK IS TO TEACH THE SIMPLEST, MOST fundamental forms of object juggling, starting with three-ball juggling. The most accessible pattern for juggling three balls—or for that matter, three of anything, be they clubs, hoops, eggs or frying pans—is called the cascade. It happens to be the basis for all advanced forms of juggling. And I propose that mastering three-ball cascade juggling is a respectable, attainable goal. Juggling objects at any level of difficulty can help a person better juggle those nettlesome though important intangibles that add gravity to daily living. Rafts of ideas, trains of thought, carloads of responsibility can be awkward, nebulous concepts that may be challenging to grasp, but keeping them circulating through a space we call the mind is largely what keeps any of us in circulation. By learning to juggle material things, physical, emotional, and intellectual abilities and sensitivities are enhanced. And with increased consciousness of expanded potentials, any juggling task becomes easier.

That may sound like a lot to look for in an activity that most people perceive as frivolous entertainment. Why, the very word juggling has suffered bad connotations for 600 years or so, but the skill, the talent, the art, whatever you want to call juggling, has been around for a long time. With the pace of change in the world accelerating exponentially, any acquired taste that lingers on the collective palate of humanity for more than a generation must have something going for it.

I suspect that you would not be reading this book if you had never picked up two or three oranges, or tennis balls, or rocks, or balled-up socks and tried to juggle. Like most people, you probably did it wrong in terms of a cascade pattern—approximating instead a more difficult "shower" pattern, which will be described in chapter thirteen, or you were so overwhelmed by the apparent complexity of juggling once objects actually become airborne that you gave up without a fair attempt—before you broke something. You might have been at least inwardly pleased if one of those first errant missiles had bopped one of the knaves who were snickering at your ungainly juggling posture. But what if you conked yourself?

Fear not! Juggling is easy! It looks harder than it is. A lot of incredibly difficult looking stunts performing jugglers use in their acts are just razzle-dazzle and showmanship. Sure, there are great jugglers, but anyone who can flip a ball up into the air and catch it on the way down can juggle. You do not have to be a genetically specialized circus star to manage this sport. With determination, patience, and time you can learn to juggle, and like roller skating or driving a car, once learned, the skill is never forgotten.

A few years ago, I worked on an assignment at an elementary school where part of my job was to teach a small group of nine- and ten-year-olds how to juggle. There was less for the kids to unlearn than there usually is for adult student jugglers, so we were able to move through preliminary steps quickly. The children were enthusiastic and attentive, and that always helps. They did not, as a group, strike me as unusually well-coordinated, and there were no exceptionally talented stand-outs in the bunch. I never expected all of them to learn the motions of a cascade pattern within fifteen minutes. It was something less than *Star Wars,* but in an hour each had controlled the flight of three rubber balls through at least a complete cascade juggling cycle of tossing and catching each ball one time. Some of the young students juggled five or six circuits the first day—and without using the part of my juggling method that truly makes juggling easy to learn, even without a private teacher.

If average ten-year-olds can learn to juggle, it is a physical certainty that the ability to juggle falls well within a range of material possibility for most mortals. Granted, some people have to work harder at it than others, but what about those grandiose claims that juggling enhances intellectual abilities and emotional potentials? How does juggling do that?

Juggling usually comes not in a flash, but in a sweat generated by discipline, determination, and a desire to achieve. Even if a basic cascade is a snap for you to master, some advanced phases of the sport, the shower pattern perhaps, or juggling four balls, or five knishes with a broom balanced on your nose, will assuredly be less easy for you to handle. Most people have to make an emotional and intellectual commitment to learn to juggle. It may take you days, or even weeks, to catch on. You may have to think about what you are doing. Paying attention as you practice, analyzing little hitches in your movements that you take for granted, and recognizing your attitudes can be crucial for, as contradictory as this may seem, juggling is as much a stance as it is an activity.

Good juggling takes bodily skill, agility, and dexterity. It does not require large size or physical aggressiveness. It wastes no motion, moves quickly outside typical modes of conscious thought to become instinctual dance, freeing up limits of strength and ability. New awareness comes from heightened sensitivity and increased flexibility. Juggling compresses energy into a concentrated way of feeling and seeing that it is possible to achieve cohesive flow, no matter how chaotic things may appear to be. And juggling is, more than anything else, fun, though perhaps only as silly and frivolous as skillful concentration, coordination, control and imagination ever are.

Juggling can help you develop a sense of ease about yourself. From that may grow self-confidence that can make you feel better about everything and undercut tension in your life. Since elementary cascade juggling is an individual activity, you can really compete only with yourself. You set your limits and goals. If you ever advance to juggling with a partner, that talent will definitely help you work better with others—or bruise you badly. But basic solo cascade juggling will just as surely teach you to work better and well with yourself. Self-reliance is a key to vitality.

And juggling slows everything down. To you, a novice, juggling looks impossibly fast-moving, but to a juggler, it all unfolds with graceful order at the ends of the hands. Most students approach this state of grace by breaking juggling into small component motions that may be mastered one at a time before being strung together. Addressing any complex activity through thorough experience of its factors makes for

a clear understanding of the whole system. This makes a once knotty challenge
more simply accessible than it had been
before, but only to those whose determination, fortitude, and patience have
carried them that far, step by step. In
this time-honoring way, becoming a
juggler may entail just the characters
that can slow the world down to manageable speed. Any juggler is a master of

gravity, but maybe the great jugglers master reality by
stopping the world for an instant while the balls are flying!

All this from juggling?

Yes, and more. Juggling approximates perfection and is
limitless. It will take you as far as you want to go toward
making the impossible real.

You can do it. JUST JUGGLE!

CHAPTER
1

Definitions

Juggling Objects

Juggling objects is the act of keeping items in motion through the air by alternately tossing and catching them. Purists insist that there must be more airborne articles than the number of hands involved, but some of the greatest jugglers might argue that the most simply eloquent juggling may be done with only two balls or just one.

Frequently juggled items include rubber balls, plastic or wooden hoops, Indian-type clubs, and ceramic plates, but virtually anything that can be thrown and caught with one hand is fair game for jugglers. Flaming batons, raw eggs, or delicate blown crystal are juggled by skilled pros who have refined their talents over the years. None of these things are recommended for the novice. Juggling can cause damage, but if treated with respect, it is not a hazardous sport in its rudimentary phases unless you are frightened by the real possibility of being clipped on the head by an off-the-mark juggling ball. Weird props make

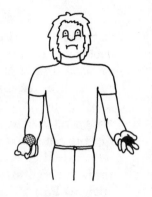

juggling difficult; however, danger and excitement provide excellent entertainment for an audience. This book will show you how to juggle for yourself—first, satisfy an audience of one.

Three-ball cascade juggling involves tossing, then tossing and catching repeatedly, in sequence, with oneself or with partners. A juggler flings one object at a time into the air until all three things that were held are incorporated into a pattern traversing paths from hand to hand through the air. Opposite pathways are normally identical in duration and something like mirror images in flight. Maintaining the sequential arrangement requires throwing and catching with one hand, then doing the same with the other, which takes concentration, and usually a fair amount of practice, to master.

To the casual observer of a three-ball cascade, all three spheres may appear to be flying at one time. In reality, only two balls are ever airborne at once, though these two balls are changed rapidly and continuously.

A juggle starts with two balls in one hand, one ball in the other. When one ball is sprung up from the hand holding two, one ball is in the air. When that ball begins to come *down,* the single ball in the opposite hand is pitched up; two balls are in the air. The first throw needs to be caught at right about this time, leaving only one ball, which is now on its way down, in the air. So the third ball must be tossed up immediately to make room in hand for the incoming ball. And then, as that last throw comes down, the first ball needs to be rethrown back toward the hand that first tossed it, beginning the reverse go-round of the initial ball-cycle for the second full circuit of a cascade sequence.

After the first throw to get the pattern moving, a ball is always pitched up by each hand just before that hand catches the previous toss from the other hand. To accomplish this state of enlightened ambidexterity, a juggler must practice throwing accurately and tuning in to fleeting visual cues, for openers. Part III of this book makes juggling easy to learn by explaining all of this in detail, one manageable, chaos-free step at a time.

Timing is critical to juggling. Slight deviations in tempo can throw a pattern off a bit at a time, so that within two or

We are all jugglers, whether we know it or want to be.

three off-beat throws an entire pattern might slip irretrievably out of control. And consistent control is another secret of juggling. Skilled performers—particularly comic jugglers—may create the appearance of disorder in their routines by juggling odd or perilous items of awkward shapes and varying sizes thrown in seemingly haphazard ways, but a talented juggler is always in command  whether juggling three live chickens (It has been done!), or a grape, a cue ball, an apple, a cabbage, and a basketball. In the instance of the latter, juggling any five items requires extremely rapid movements which make regimentation mandatory. There is considerably less leeway for error when juggling five objects than there would be when more slowly juggling three things, where mistakes can sometimes be compensated for by quick action that keeps a slightly altered pattern flowing. Juggling five things demands split-second timing and pin-point accuracy which do not easily lend themselves to improvisation. Find someone who can juggle five of anything and watch the quickness, agile dexterity, and focused strength it takes to be a silly juggler.

Juggling Intangibles

Over years, juggling has taken on other meanings beside sportive. Some have been unkind—many people think of juggling as devious manipulation to reach a desired end. But any management to accomplish flow is juggling, and in modern society we are all jugglers whether we know it or want to be.

A father with a crying baby in one arm, dinner burning on the stove, another child dismantling the next room, the phone ringing, and a Girl Scout at the door waiting to be paid for cookies is a juggler.

A businesswoman with important papers to read and sign yesterday, her spouse on one phone, her broker on another, her lover on her knee, and a luncheon to attend a half hour ago to give the guest speech is a juggler.

It is four P.M., Joe College is on his way to a final exam. Joe's English Lit term paper is due in the morning and still unwritten. Joe's gal Sal finished her last test already and will be leaving at eight A.M. for a summer job with the Peace Corps in Bangladesh. Joe will not see Sal again until the fall term. He is a juggler with a mission.

Men and women juggle jobs, families, dreams, feelings, responsibilities, hungers, and better judgments all the time. Even children juggle enthusiasm for play, curiosity, developing physical and mental abilities, parental attentions, and peer pressures everyday.

We all juggle, though some of us are more naturally skilled at it than others. Multitudes just slog through muddled lives. Inexactitudes, misjudgments, sloppy transits, and mournful endings make up good days. At times, we may feel hard-pressed to keep one idea or niggling responsibility from crashing to the ground and dragging us down with it in ruins. But a juggler routinely keeps three, or four, or more things flying and, what may be more impressive, achieves a form near perfection to boot.

With no way to practice living lives filled with activity and commitment, it is a wonder that worldly conditions are only as hectic as they are. Rarely, if ever, do many of us come close to order, let alone perfection. Competition is fierce in the work-place, pressure is intense. Leisure-oriented diversions from hot-air ballooning, to hot-tubbing, to hot-oil massage are popular ways of filling spare time, as more and more people do something besides being bombarded by video in

their time-off. People are on the go because they want to be, or because they
cannot sit still, or because they fear
private demons will catch them if they
stop, but legions do it poorly.

Stress is epidemic. Chronic anxiety
states, obesity, high blood pressure,
heart disease, ulcers, and strokes are
common pay-offs for keeping busy badly.
Medical experts agree that emotional
factors, not purely physical ones, contribute to these conditions. Short-fused tempers lit by angry frustration are by-
products of the tension people operate under everyday.
The hyperstressed are our poorest jugglers.

We all need to juggle jobs, responsibilities, thoughts, emotions, and actions anyway, so why not do it well? Sure, things
are happening fast, but that is no warrant for sloppy laziness.

Because everyone is worrying about what to do next, no
one has time to think about what do now. Everybody is busy
playing with funds and with feelings, buying into this ratio-
nale or that religion, investing precious energy in a thousand
large and small excuses. People feel pressured into believing
there is only time to react, and the only logical reaction to
confusion and insanity is irrationality. The fretful thought
that we could do better is hard to shake off. And yet it is
much more convenient to stumble through another day without pesky ideas about excellence, mastering commitments,
bargaining with destiny, or thriving. We know that few of us
will ever be concert pianists or hirsute rock stars, few will
win an Academy Award or smack homers out of Yankee
Stadium. These realizations are part of maturity, and insensi-
bility is a hopeless retort to aging. Instead of obliterating
receding youthful ideals, it might be better to turn them inward, to continue to dream.

Holding It Up

Anyone who can throw and catch a ball in his or her hand can juggle. This makes juggling a modest goal in a complex world—a simple dream, but nonetheless a joust with complacency for mastery of a corner of the self that can make you feel good. Juggling can teach you that there are ways to look at hard-to-keep-track-of options to create a cohesive, unified, manageable whole system from them, if you consider individual aspects one by one with no initial regard for the large complex whatsoever.

Building a brick house is a massive undertaking. It boggles my mind to think about all that goes into one structure. I cannot imagine the complete brilliance that can conceive and produce a brick house. But if I first consider the foundation, a hole that must be dug, and cement that must be poured; and if I satisfy my curiosity about that phase of construction before moving on to study the framework, the floors, the walls, and the rest, step by manageable step, pretty soon the house starts looking simpler. Then it starts looking possible. The finished house is not magic. It is perseverance forged of thoughtful choices pieced together to establish a new unity, the highest form of communion, a marriage work of concentrated desires.

Juggling objects is not magic either. It is a skillful coordination, poise and balance put together step by step, piece by tiny piece to form a systematically integrated juggling routine. Taken in its entirety, the action of a juggler may seem disconcertingly complex, but difficult forms are composed of smaller bits. And it is around these elements that learning takes place. To learn juggling, component actions are best examined individually, practiced separately, mastered one by one, until all the aspects that make up a juggling pattern are under your control. At that point you may exultantly look forward to juggling success beyond beginner's luck.

An interesting thing happens when all the pieces start to fall into place. You see at once that juggling is not so perplexing, not so intricate that it cannot be approached; juggling is easy to do once the parts that comprise it are clarified and mastered. An activity that seemed too formidable to understand becomes something that can be done well at any level of accomplishment. And on reach- 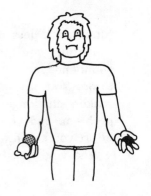 ing one level, you can always go beyond it, not necessarily to greater juggling feats, but to the other side of flirtation with perfection.

Beyond excellence, beyond experience of doing anything with utmost competence is freedom from pressure to achieve. After considerable practice of the three-ball cascade, your grasp of it may be such that you will find that conscious thought about juggling actually interferes with your perfor- mance. At that point you will have discovered an athlete's consummation of movement keyed to reflexes and instinct. In the flow of a juggling routine, bits of moving business occur faster than you can think about them, but if they have been mastered separately, they will be recalled subconsciously as they need to be.

So you find yourself juggling. The apparently impossible is real, it is happening. You are doing something that you never thought you could do before; you are bringing order into a turbulent, imperfect world. Now, everything seems simpler. Life looks more manageable because poise, balance, and dex- terity—the very skills sharpened by juggling three balls—are conveniently applicable to real life situations. Performing at work, pleasing your partner or anyone you care for, patiently helping your kids do homework, bathing your hound after it just rolled in another dog's poo, raking the yard, getting the car inspected, dealing with all the daily hubbub, ad infinitum, seems less overwhelming. Success at learning to do something you thought impossible has given you a shot of confidence in your ability to accomplish whatever you set out to do. You have realized how to look at the elements that make a challenge complex rather than at an entire crushing problem, and you know that through diligent, determined effort you can prevail.

And you thought juggling was a frivolous diversion.

CHAPTER
2

History

Egyptian hieroglyphics depict female jugglers on pyramid walls and ancient histories of Oriental, Indian and Native American cultures include recorded counterparts to juggling in various forms. The modern word *juggle,* however, is rooted in the Latin, *joculari* — meaning to jest or to joke — and one branch of juggling's roots may be traced back to fifty years before the birth of Christ.

Julius Caesar and fellow Romans delighted in viewing games of endurance and skill. Roman circuses evolved as showcases for gladitorial combat, animal sacrifices, human slaughter, and other less deadly entertainments, including nonlethal sporting events. For example, to float mock naval battles, the Roman Colosseum was flooded. As a sidelight to these extravaganzas from which modern circuses derived, magicians, acrobats, and jugglers performed for crowds in excess of 100,000 people.

With the expansion of the Roman Empire, so spread performers to the hinterlands, playing for even greater audiences coming to see ever more magnificent entertainments, such as chariot races, Olympiads, human versus lion competitions, and so on.

As the Empire faded, the demands for huge amphitheater shows dimmed. When the Roman Empire fell in 476, the arenas closed down for good, and many performers, without stages to play on, became itinerants, traveling from town to town in quest of a gig. They played where they could, at town squares and meeting places, for coins, a meal, or a place to sleep.

For centuries the fate of actors, acrobats, mimes, and jugglers was to wander. By the Middle Ages, these enduring talents had evolved in two directions for survival. A street theater tradition featuring jugglers, tightrope walkers, acrobatic tumblers, and performers of balancing acts spread throughout Europe. Concurrently, a custom of minstrels, singers, and story-tellers arose. These tale-spinners found versatility to their benefit, and practiced varied skills. Reciting poetry, doing acrobatics and juggling were common aptitudes. The most renowned of these performers were called in to formal assemblies to perform for reigning monarchs and nobles, and the most popular of these players were invited to stay on as private retainers. These were the first court jesters.

Initially, court minstrels sang of heroic deeds, but tastes for minstrelsy declined and singers were forced to change their tunes to hold onto their jobs. Minstrels became jokers to humor their bosses; where they once sang of bravery, newly enfranchised clowns displayed sometimes pointed wit. The wearing of funny, patchwork clothing festooned with bells and dangling animal ears was meant to cement their positions as fools, but these servants also continued to practice traditional dancing, acrobatic and juggling skills as parts of their acts. Perhaps the *foolish* connotations of these arts that persist in certain circles today derive straight from this time. What people little remember about

those early jesters is that they had special access to the inner power circles of their time. As long as they provided laughs, their guise as simpletons granted them immunity from punishment for saying things to ruling monarchs that less entertaining subjects could never get away with.

Through the Middle Ages, no organized circuses existed. Asia, Europe, and Africa hosted itinerant performers who played wherever people met—at community celebrations and market squares. Rope-walker riggings often hung from church steeples, which were the most substantial structures many towns had to offer. Musical recitals and theatrical productions put on by touring groups in the open air drew crowds from far and wide.

By the 1400s, competition among traveling performers had become fierce. Unscrupulous operators sought to enhance receipts by adding sleight-of-hand magic and conjuring to their stable of talents, and a respected dextrous skill took on a less than attractive meaning. The blow that juggling's reputation suffered still smarts. Manipulations with a decidedly deceitful bent became associated with the talent and with the very word for it, such as in the enduring phrase "juggling the books."

To combat an increasingly negative image, performers regrouped; players banded together. And by the 1700s, when clowns, tightrope artists, jugglers, equestrians, and animal handlers brought their acts to the American frontier, tent-show circuses were popular amusements in most parts of the world. Many of these traditions persist today. Russian acrobatic troupes boast world record holding jugglers who are national heroes in a homeland where gymnastics, tumbling, balancing, and juggling are disciplines studied from childhood. There are 20,000 professional acrobats in China, where eight-year-olds are tested in rhythm, balance, flexibility, strength, endurance, reaction time, and academics for recruitment into state-supported performing troupes. Some oriental performers are able to balance stacks of cups and saucers on their heads while riding unicycles on tabletops. Others juggle glasses filled with water without spilling a drop.

American and European circuses still travel the world over, and although there are relatively few shows today, those that have survived are mainly large ones. Tents are rarely used, having been replaced by immovable auditoriums which house today's versions of Colosseum-like spectacles, minus the most blatant violence, of course, in these eminently civilized times. The jugglers are still there. Maybe they double as clowns, or perhaps they are part of a family act fulfilling a performing heritage—a brother and sister passing clubs back and forth from atop their juggling parents' shoulders, exactly as the elders did when they were children.

Juggling is rhythm, and the beat goes on—even in unlikely places, such as on the island of Tonga in the South Pacific, where juggling is a native tradition with a twist: Only women on Tonga juggle.

Throughout the South Seas, natives of Fiji, the Gilbert Islands and Samoa have long juggled local nuts and fruits, but the lady jugglers of Tonga may be the most accomplished of all. Favorite props are plentiful tui-tui nuts (similar to chestnuts) and limes, of which ten-year-old schoolgirls can commonly juggle five. Seven is considered a more respectable number, and Tongan women demonstrate their aptitude with extremely hard to control juggling patterns rising fifteen to twenty feet into the air. Apparently, juggling was long ago part of a ritual revolving around the brewing of a locally popular narcotic drink called Kava. Furthermore, at one time, the greater a Tongan woman's juggling skills, the better her chances of marrying a wealthy, landed Tongan gentleman were.

There are even current counterparts to the itinerant performers of the Middle Ages in the street performers of the eighties. San Francisco has them, so does New York, and Boulder, Colorado. In these and other cities (see chapter fifteen), exuberantly talented, mostly youthful players sim-

ply set a stage on any busy street, plaza or courtyard, much the same way as their olden counterparts did hundreds of years ago. There, musical or magical or juggling acts go on without schedules to trade a few coins for a smiling moment of pleased astonishment.

Skilled Jugglers and Rare Feats

Unknown jugglers have collected spare change for centuries, but behind the usual anonymity of such performers are several well-known jugglers whose feats in recent times have helped juggling survive as a modern art. One of the most famous, though not for his juggling expertise, was W. C. Fields, the comedian.

Fields began juggling fruits and vegetables at his father's produce stand at age nine, and from there went on to vaudeville where his original act consisted of juggling cigar boxes, croquet balls, and Indian clubs, punctuated by acerbic commentary, witticisms, and the noted Fields sarcasm. It was not until later in his career that Fields became an actor-film star. And even then, in the thirties and forties, when he was a bankable Hollywood asset, he always included juggling in his act. The call for stage show juggling was silent by that time, but Fields' motion pictures feature some of the best and most

famous juggling scenes ever recorded. Classic films, such as *The Pool Shark* (1915) and *The Old Fashioned Way* (1934), display Fields' talents at balancing a top hat on the tip of a cane, doing stick tricks with the cane, such as dropping it to the ground and making it spring back into his hand, or remarkably toe-flipping the cane from foot to foot. The tools of the trade, a top hat and

cane, became Fields' trademarks just as clearly as did his red-nosed, side-of-the-mouth punchline delivery. It is hard to measure how much of Fields' appeal came from his comically imprecise physical orientation to an ever annoying world, but the grumpy, blustering, shambling persona was an act made possible by the honed techniques of the juggler's skills. Rhythm, finesse, and ultimately incredible harmony of motion were the underpinnings of Fields' genuine artistry.

Many other films besides Fields' have had juggling sequences. Buster Keaton performed a surrealistic juggle in a film in which he portrayed a juggler trying to win a talent contest on a radio program. Chaplin cascaded a salami, a hunk of cheese, and a loaf of bread in *The Circus* in 1928. *Charlie Chan at the Circus* (1936), *The Marx Brothers at The Circus* (1939—Harpo juggled), and *Casablanca* (1942) fea-

ture jugglers mostly in background settings. *The Greatest Show on Earth* (1952—Academy Award winning Best Picture of the Year) has some great juggling, including a woman floor-bouncing five balls, and *The Juggler* (1953) starred Kirk Douglas in the title role for which he performed his own juggling stunts. *Our Man Flint* (1966), *Animal House* (1977), and *The Jerk* (1980) have juggling scenes, the latter memorable for a cat-juggling sequence featuring on outrageous three-cat cascade and a brief two-cats in one-hand clockwise cyclic juggle. Nevertheless, aficionados and experts agree that W. C. Fields is the greatest of the screen jugglers so far.

Another notable juggler was Chrys Holt, who was with the Ringling Brothers, Barnum and Bailey Circus. Demure Miss Holt captured audiences' attention by climbing gracefully up a special rigging designed for her act. Just below the peak of the big-top tent above the center ring, she juggled for the crowd, but only after she was securely hanging from her long, knotted hair. Suspended above the sawdust and the gasping viewers, Chrys really wowed 'em in the fifties. Although such antics are not recommended for standard issue human beings, Chrys Holt apparently established standards for her field; the 1982 Ringling Brothers show features young Margarite Michel who juggles flame torches while she swings in the air from her long hair.

Through the early sixties, jugglers continued to appear in

INTRODUCTION

films, Las Vegas revues, and such places as the *Ed Sullivan Show* and circuses. But circuses became fewer and fewer, and TV-variety showcases went off the air. Street performers carried the juggling tradition through the late sixties and the seventies, giving impetus for the eighties to performers like Michael Davis, an ex-San Francisco street juggler, and the Flying Karamazov

Brothers, four young jugglers whose night-club act proves that juggling has more than real staying power — their enlivened shows demonstrate what jesters and jugglers have known for centuries, namely, jugglers are nobody's fools.

Far removed from the silent, puffy-sleeved, rhinestone-studded, circus-style, Las Vegas-type jugglers many of us are used to seeing, the Karamazovs, not really brothers, not even Russians but from California, are one of the best juggling teams in the world, according to the International Jugglers Association. Using perceptive topical humor as a back-drop for skillfully entertaining feats, the brothers fling torches and axes back and forth at each other, risking real danger in the process. A mistake while juggling a running chainsaw (!) would be no laughing matter, so you know these guys are good. And they continually expand jugglers' horizons. Balls, hoops, and clubs are perfect items for most jugglers to play with, but the Karamazovs are not contented with the ordinary. Though they sometimes use standard juggling props, they also like to toss bottles of liquor, musical instruments, live animals, and sickles at each other. Even after a display of the brothers' dexterous versatility, audiences are usually surprised by the troupe's challenging finale to their act when one of them offers to juggle any three items the audience wishes to provide. If he succeeds, they are to present him with a standing ovation; if he fails, he promises to accept a pie in the face. It is not easy to juggle a slinky, a kite, and a birthday cake. The pie was the reward that night, but the evening he was handed a prophylactic, an overcoat, and a bag of kitty litter he got the applause.

Unlike the Karamazovs, juggler Michael Davis works solo. His big break came when he landed a job on the Great White Way in a show called *Broadway Follies*. Although Davis told jokes, played the guitar, sang, balanced hats and canes, and juggled five balls ending in a neck catch before being chased around the stage by a dog, the show folded on opening night. Despite the setback, he quickly moved into another Broadway show, a more successful revue called *Sugar Babies*, where he attracted attention juggling hatchets and cleavers, as well as a bowling ball, with an apple and a raw egg which ended up in his mouth! Davis has been the subject of a Dick Cavett interview on PBS where he juggled three ping-pong balls with his mouth only, and has made numerous appearances on the *Saturday Night Live* TV show. For the latter, he did a juggling routine to demonstrate a danger of Halloween on an October 31 program. Showing how easily razor blades could be inserted into trick-or-treaters' apples, Davis studded two pieces of fruit with blades before juggling both in one hand. Then he added a third plain apple and juggled all three in a variety of cascades, reverse cascades, and shower patterns before devouring the bladeless fruit by bringing it up to his mouth each time it landed in his right hand and taking gobbling bites out of it without breaking the juggling sequence. He was really sharp that night.

Tomorrow's History

Juggling today is experiencing ever growing interest all over the world. Europe, Russia, and China are hotbeds of juggling activity. Juggling clubs abound throughout the United States (see chapter sixteen), where beginners may pick up basic instruction and more advanced jugglers may find partners to juggle with and swap tricks. And juggling has become a craze on college campuses from MIT to Stanford where experimental mathematicians and engineers are attracted to its controllable outcome. Remembering that Yale students flung the first Frisbie Pie Co. tins that lent their name to the plastic discs  that became part of world-wide sports-consciousness, it seems only a matter of time before the juggling bug filters out into mainstream culture where an expectant populous is likely to catch it. By 1990, I think people will be juggling in office hallways and at bus stops. Juggling will be taught in elementary schools, and high schools and colleges will sponsor competitive juggling events. Shopping malls are already holding popular, crowd-pleasing juggling marathons to raise money for charities. And why not? There must be some power to juggling for it to have endured as an amusement for more than 5,000 years. It is fun, of course. But it must also be more; there has to be something special about a basically repetitive activity that has attracted performers and audiences for centuries.

People may be fascinated by juggling because plates, and clubs, and slinkies flying through the air seems like magic, and who cannot use a bit of that in his life? The larger question is: Why rely on happenstance, on seeing a show, on stumbling onto a magical wire-walking street juggler, or on waiting for the circus to come to town, for juggling to be done for you? It is greater fun to be a juggler than it is to watch one. So why be a spectator when you can control your own magic just as surely as you can control the rhythm of the balls?

The future is in your hands.

JUST JUGGLE!

PART
II

Why Juggle?

ANY QUEST FOR KNOWLEDGE IS STIMULATING. THE ANTICIPA-
tion of knowing is exciting. Thinking about what it would be
like to juggle may be similar to imagining a first orgasm for a
person who has never had one; the objective seems like an
end in and of itself—the highest level attainable. But it is
really a beginning, a door to another state of consciousness.
Learning to juggle is like learning the alphabet: From it you
can create a new vocabulary for self-expression. And juggling
touches all aspects of your being. It can make your body,
brain, and heart work better and feel great.

CHAPTER
3

Physical Benefits

Juggling can help your body feel sound from head to toe. It can teach your eyes to see in unaccustomed ways and strengthen your shoulders, arms, wrists, and hands. The sport may enhance and sharpen your senses of touch, hearing, taste, and smell. And juggling can produce these and other physical benefits without great strain to your body.

Exercise

Juggling is a relatively gentle exercise that emphasizes coordination over strength. It tones your body instead of tiring it, starting right at the top with your eyes.

At first glance, fast-flying juggling balls appear to be untraceable blurs, making juggling patterns impossible to comprehend completely. That we normally trust our eyesight, relying on it for perhaps an inordinate amount of sensory input, is the problem. If our vision falters, we may feel lost. But jugglers must see what they are doing. Their eyes need to discriminate based on minimal visual information.

Trying to follow things moving simultaneously in different directions can be hopelessly disorienting, so a juggler's eyes need to learn to track rapidly moving objects without looking directly at them. This is done by controlling the pathways of the objects, finding a spot all the paths have in common, keying on it, and predicting from there where else the props will travel. Exercises in chapter ten describe ways to relax your eyes. With such techniques, which may help you follow and manage a juggling pattern with only glimmers of visual stimulation for reference, you may learn to see more clearly.

As you become less dependent on sight, other senses may evolve to pick up slack in the information chain. Touch may become sharper from sensing the shape and size of juggling balls—what hefting force you need to toss them and what grip you need to catch. Sensitive hearing may tune you in to the rhythmic slap of the balls on your palms, help you locate noisy rolling or bouncing misses, and can even clue you in to things you cannot see your drops breaking. Taste and smell enhancement may be stretching juggling's physical benefits, but for the standard jugglers' bit of eating an apple juggled along with two balls it is useful to develop taste buds sensitive enough to prevent you from trying to eat a ball. And a sharp sense of smell may be helpful for avoiding rotten produce that might be thrown *at* you if you blow the apple trick (or any other) in front of a rowdy audience. A good sixth sense to duck when necessary may also be enhanced by juggling.

Moving past senses and nonsenses, your shoulders and

arms will get a workout from juggling. These parts are not supposed to move much while you juggle, but they anchor the real juggling works, your wrists and hands. Juggling for even one minute may pain untrained shoulders and arms, but happily, by the time you are skilled enough to juggle for a minute, you probably will have had to practice enough to be fit for it.

At the end of the strong arms, a juggler's wrists work differently from those used for throwing a baseball or football. In ordinary throwing, a wrist snaps, but the wrist does not "break" to make juggling throws; it controls a cupped hand by directing an upward thrusting of the palm to spring a ball out of it. Then, to catch, your juggler's hands will need to respond quickly to moving patterns, sensitively and surely grabbing throws in perfect time without the luxury of eyesight showing you where the balls are.

From the waist down, a good cascade juggler should be immobile. It is extradifficult to keep track of flying juggling balls while worrying about tripping over your feet. The discipline of restricting unnecessary motion may help you center your energies where they are most needed—in your hands and eyes. Later, as your skills improve, you may move any part of your body, doing over-the-shoulder, behind-the-back, and under-the-leg throws, and catches with grace and agility that people will call style. But it is best not to rush things; learn to juggle first. Style will emerge.

These exercise factors make juggling more of a toning activity than a strenuous one. Juggling can provide invigorating, yet gently controllable, release, instead of exhaustion as it coaxes broader vision from your eyes and nudges ever more accurate throws and catches from your hands. Because juggling is not so much a test as a direction, slowly, as you catch on to it, your body stretches past tired old limits, slyly building strength and vigor along a way that points toward a gracefully efficient manner, which can make you feel good and especially light.

But juggling may seem like unusual movement. Simply coordinating both hands may be foreign to you unless you are ambidextrous, or at least extremely versatile at patting your head while rubbing your stomach—with either hand in either position. Initial powerlessness in your own hand, even if it is a subordinate one, can be disheartening, but juggling may eventually equalize the strengths in your hands. With practice, a juggler pushes a disused hand beyond self-limiting behavior into spheres never touched before. Disturbing weakness is patiently replaced by enlivening ability as two hands evolve into a balanced unit.

As you become more perceptive and competent, picture this: Your hands are springing, flinging, and catching balls. There is barely time for you to see visual fragments of balls flashing along the farthest edges of your vision, let alone time to think about them, but you can catch the balls cleanly by sensing their positions in flight and keeping the pattern moving precisely. This is what it feels like to be alert to a new variety of subtle sensory cues. Balanced coordination can be learned; juggling teaches it through training and exercise.

Coordination

Juggling develops coordination. A juggler's synchronized reflexes reflect balanced external and internal organization which can help produce a ready, loose and warmed-up body. Feeling good in such ways may benefit musicians, athletes, theatrical performers, or most who work with and care about their bodies—executives, job interviewees, schoolchildren, mothers, fathers, just about everyone else, and especially anyone who operates under stress to perform on cue.

Juggling might help a musician or an actor warm up, instead of walking on stage to perform cold. A player could harmonize reflexes and timing with the rhythm of the balls before a show, and such fine-tuning—as well as a sense of wonder that juggling seems to inherently impart—might prepare and tone harmlessly when compared with more common mood enhancers such as drugs and  alcohol. And a musician or an actor lucky enough to have a juggling partner in the band or company would be able to work toward twining joint sensibilities, binding coordinated skills into a sensitively sympathetic greater unit.

Athletes might benefit from a few minutes of juggling before a competition. A boxer might banish prefight jitters by juggling—by getting juices flowing without expending too much precious energy prior to the opening bell. Ballplayers, tennis players, swimmers, golfers, bowlers, and acrobats might likewise benefit by composing their timing and strength. Video arcade athletes might sharpen their hand-eye coordination for better performance at computerized sports. And even failed athletes might at last find a sport at which they can practice and excel without need for a giant body or superhuman strength.

After a few minutes' juggling, executives might better arrange their energies for a memorable level gaze and firm handshake before an important meeting.

After a rough day with the kids, a mother or father might regain self-possession in a brief juggling work-out. Parents of infants might learn to use their subordinate hands by juggling, and function in better balance with a babe in arms.

Harried clerks might take juggling breaks to adapt a patient smile for facing more customers.

Artists and writers might add a new resource to their arsenals for removing creative blocks by juggling to clear clouded visions and structure a handy work flow.

The unemployed might benefit more than most from juggling by learning to focus energy on coming to grips with employment challenges. With much time on their hands, some jobless people might practice juggling for long hours, possibly solving an employment dilemma by becoming skilled enough to turn pro!

And most children are able to learn to juggle as soon as they can throw and catch a ball. Since self-confidence may be enhanced through positive body awareness, if juggling were taught in grade schools, children might benefit by learning a noncompetitive, nonviolent way to become coordinated and feel good about their little bodies.

Newly apportioned dexterity and sharpened vision might prove helpful for performing better dentistry, surgery, carpentry, paper-hanging, haircutting, bartending, or any task calling for hand-to-hand or hand-to-eye coordination. Any active person can approach a beneficial individual symmetry by working to become synchronized with the rhythm of the balls.

Drops

Everyone who juggles needs to drill in basics. Training is paramount for juggling success. Some pros rehearse eight hours daily, and one of the prime components of practice for pros and beginners alike can actually be the most strenuous exercise you may encounter in juggling—namely, chasing drops. Every juggler misses frequently when learning something new. But if you want to juggle, with patience and faith, eventually you will triumph over confusion. Meanwhile, accepting drops as a functional part of the juggling process may be crucial to your ultimate proficiency.

Depending on what you are juggling, misses can be problems. Clubs do not bounce well or far away, but they are fairly difficult to learn to juggle with. Rings are relatively easy to juggle, but they have limited adaptability and can roll for a long time. Bean bags are good to work with. They, too, are somewhat limited by the range of tricks you may use them for, but they do not bounce at all. And neither do eggs, plates, chickens, kittens, or chainsaws, but they are not easy for beginners to juggle. Rubber balls, which I suggest you learn to juggle with, will give you the most well-rounded combination of versatility and handling ease, even though they are made to wander. On a hard surface, juggling balls can bounce well and roll quickly out of sight.

As the balls begin to fly away, you will instinctively try to pick them up. Turning this way and that, lunging, reaching, grabbing forward and back at the bounding spheres, you may find yourself dizzyingly lurching in more directions than you ever thought existed—it may seem in all ways at the same time. Too often you may find yourself moving vainly as a ball skitters deeply away from your outstretched fingers, insinuating itself under a massive piece of furniture or a sticker bush. Too often your bravest attempts to secure the balls for just one more maddening try at this insanity called juggling may be frustratingly not enough. You may be concentrating as hard as you can, but the damn balls are still scattering all over the place! It may seem as if you are spending more time chasing drops than you are with balls in your hands.

Welcome to juggling! This is what it is all about: A juggler perches on the edge of chaos, courting disaster at the tips of the fingers, cleverly manipulating almost willful missiles to keep them flying. Watching someone else do the same thing is called entertainment. But this is one of the ways juggling demonstrates that there is never challenging growth without risk.

Yet drops interrupt the flow of a practice session. Crouching and reaching out to fetch fleeing juggling balls are real distractions, and not entertaining at all, but dealing with them can show you if you have the right stuff it takes to become a juggler. Drops are unavoidable. If you can accept that premise, you may save yourself from useless, damaging pressure that might make you underestimate and devalue your truly blooming skills.

Of course, there will always be students who are routinely hampered in their trysts with juggling because they cannot cope with missing. Some people may be afraid of failure; others may fear looking silly, or awkward or, being hurt. But any stubborn excuse that prevents you from experiencing juggling in the here and now is foolish. Fearful droppers who will not let go of what they have convinced themselves they already know may be the most difficult students to teach.

There are no absolute rights or wrongs in juggling. A juggler need not be perfect to have fun, and one's image as a human being does not rest on how well one can juggle. Everyone misses, and drops may be put to your advantage if you learn to relish the bending and stooping as chances to take a break from maintaining a constant rhythm. Interruptions let you catch your breath, stretch your arms and legs, flex your midsection, and enjoy a brief, restful pause from the action. And picking up stray balls is exercise; every bow is a body strengthener. So misses can even get you fit and trim.

As you get further into juggling, drops may also help you gauge your progress. Try spearing bounding misses on one hop. Lunge for them; it is really great for hand-eye coordina-

WHY JUGGLE?

tion. Each day you will snag balls you would have missed the day before. Soon, interruptions to the juggling flow will be minimized as your reactions become more assured. And the quicker you get, the more risks you may be willing to take. Spinning around quickly to reach behind your back for a projectile you *hear* bounding away, you may note that your balance is better, your peripheral vision sharper, your hearing increasingly accurate. You may  trust your hands, your eyes, and your ears more than ever before. And drops will not set you back as far as they once did, since various body parts will be working closely together, more quickly in the instant when you react to a miss than you might once have thought possible. Glancing out of the corner of your eye, sighting a shadow of a ball before it is lost, and reaching, snagging, and holding it, even while spotting another sphere bouncing away and grabbing that one too, will be within your range. You may snatch bounding balls from odd positions, and you may do so without dizziness, even without losing the juggling beat. You will realize that drops are no longer problems; they are part of the flow! And by channeling energy into handling many things at once, you can approach excellent coordination from head to toe, including one more part we have not specifically mentioned—your mind. Coordination of your mind with your body is what minimizes drops and makes juggling happen.

There are more benefits than factors of the flesh that can be yours if you JUST JUGGLE!

CHAPTER
4

Intellectual Benefits

Few people can pick up three balls and juggle immediately. Those rare ones who can are naturals who may soon have to seek greater juggling goals than mastering the basic cascade. But for most people, learning to juggle is a conscious process of physical exercises directed by self-control, concentration, poise, and mental balance. These qualities may have wide-ranging applications in the world beyond the balls.

Self-Control, Concentration, and Poise

In the beginning, juggling is a solitary discipline. Your body struggles against gravity because you want it to, but it takes more than manual dexterity and sharp vision to juggle. It takes mental discipline to make a juggler, and if juggling improves functions of hands and eyes, it can also sharpen qualities of mind.

Can you remember the first time you tried to ride a two-wheeler? It may have seemed like an impossible task. Turning the pedals with your feet while steering with your hands and trying to stay perpendicular to the ground was just too much to think about at one time. The machine was so wobbly! How could anyone stay up?

But people ride bikes with ease, and you probably discovered after a few scraped knees and many near catastrophic collisions and *drops* that you could do it too. It took a lot of practice, but once you established necessary self-control you were able to concentrate and achieve flow by becoming poised in what had been an awkward position.

Juggling is a lot like bike riding in that the process of learning to do it may be difficult, tiresome, and frustrating. Either objective may seem maddeningly out of reach at times, but anger, worry, greed, hunger, or distraction by any external concerns beyond the reality of the task will only make progress more elusive. You cannot learn to ride a bike or to juggle without paying strict attention to what you are doing.

Juggling, however, is its own reward, and more. The first time you juggle, just like the first time you rode a bike, you may feel like you are being taken for a ride. Of course, you are controlling the apparatus, but you may not quite know how you are doing it—only that it is happening. It can make you feel magically accomplished and weightless, and, though the magic fades, your new skills give you freedom to get where you want to go.

In a world of space shuttles, soaring crime, resource depletion, and designer jeans, it is difficult to find plain values to focus on. Unlike such impersonal concerns and a complex faith in consensus material reality that they represent, juggling is a simple exercise and a clear focal frame for concentration and the powers it grants. A juggler self-confidently holds sway over gravity—and that may be the sort of ability you need to help you stand poised to grasp the next goal that you thought you might never reach for.

This poise is the same stuff you need when a barrage of rubber balls has you dodging and feinting, as if you were in training for the Golden Gloves instead of learning to juggle. Poise is the ability to handle stress gracefully and rudimentary stages of juggling may actually be a wee bit stressful. Balls moving every conceivable way at once, in the air, off the wall, and on the ground can overwhelm a student juggler who may wish to bail out of target range and leave the juggling to the ghost of W. C. Fields.

Early on, the sport may seem more than impossible; it may seem to be a foolishly dangerous test of pride. At such moments, poise may help you recognize that causes are not lost for seeming bleak, and that the ability to concentrate on the basics of physical and mental coordination can be a solid building block that you can trust to stand under any pressure. If you pursue juggling intently, plug on and fight those rearing impulses to quit in a huff by chucking it all on the spot. Before you know what hit you—hopefully not too many stray props—you will be juggling and finding out that it is possible for order to emerge from chaos tempered with self-control. Then you will have glimpsed the flip side of confusion, where a composed state of mind and body makes you steady, ready, and wholly better balanced to roll with any curves that life may throw you.

Mental Balance

A precious state of equilibrium between smooth motion and controlled thought is possible in juggling, and this fine sense of mental and physical coordination might be what makes the sport intoxicating. The work of life may be sustaining flow between inner needs and outer environments, making the art of living maintaining that flow in a balance which integrates diverse elements in a most coherent, least stressful manner. Balance is simply the highest refinement of motion, thought, concentration, or life forces; balanced things work as best they can.

Think of the hands of a juggler. Neither may be more important than the other. Both hands must work well alone and together as a unit. A strong hand cannot compensate for a weaker one. Two hands need to work closely, as nearly equally as possible.

The essence of handedness lies not in the body but in the brain, and ours are divided into hemispheres that do different things. For starters, the right side of a human brain operates the left hand, the left brain controls the right hand, and whichever hand you favor generally corresponds with the tendencies most people have toward predominant reliance on function of one half of the brain over the other. Right-handed people tend to be more commonly left brain dominant than left-handed people, and vice-versa.

These dominances relate to how we see things. A dominant left brain favors orderliness, verbal and mathematical skills, logical-linear-reasoned thought, and any sequential learning skills. It is time related and objective. The left brain strives to make rational order out of chaos by following a proverbial "train of thought" to reach a definite solution.

Imagination is seated in the right side of the brain, the hemisphere that also controls spatial orientation, visual perceptions, metaphorical and comparative talents, intuition, fantasizing, and imagery. Musical abilities, drawing skills, creativity, appreciation of shapes and forms are all positioned in the right hemisphere.

Although there is constant interaction between the hemispheres, each half of a brain seems to influence different behavior at different times. In practice, we often simply accept current preferences toward typically right brain or left brain modes of thinking without trying to tap our potential to use a whole brain. This may be why artists have agents,

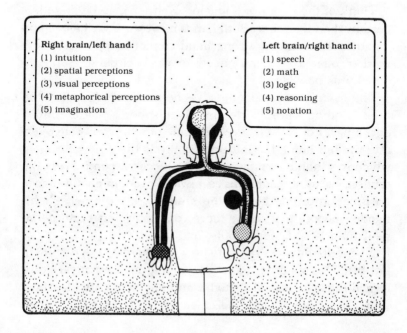

Right brain/left hand:
(1) intuition
(2) spatial perceptions
(3) visual perceptions
(4) metaphorical perceptions
(5) imagination

Left brain/right hand:
(1) speech
(2) math
(3) logic
(4) reasoning
(5) notation

authors have publishers, and everyone has a broker and wants a maid.

Juggling may be a way to combine and balance traits of both sides of the brain which are sometimes challenging to reconcile. The right brain notices and fancies juggling. The left brain logically determines a juggling pattern. The right brain creates the pattern's shape in space. The left brain maintains an orderly alternating sequence of right-hand (left brain), left-hand (right brain) motion, and which motion is largely right brain controlled. In all, the left brain provides logical information which the right brain uses to create juggling. Meshing ordinarily divergent functions of the brain may increase skills on both sides of the brain.

Two brain halves have to work effortlessly together to take bits of information and mix them in novel ways to reach a new synthesis of understanding. A juggler must handle relationships of balls to balls, balls to hands, balls to eyes, eyes to hands, and perhaps most revealingly, hand to hand, and must be able to combine and multiply these relationships by ever-changing images and experiences of these images. Juggling between a right and left hand reflects a corresponding interchange between a left and right brain. This may be simply the most persuasive evidence of juggling's potential to balance hemispheric interaction and to enhance your capabilities to deal equitably with anything you use your brain for—from directing the tangible reality of the juggling balls to handling less concrete matters affecting your life daily.

Practice for Juggling the Incorporeal

Day-by-day responsibilities and affairs weigh heavily on most of us at one time or another. Small- and large-scale perplexities and disasters such as inflation, recession, or nuclear chit-chat may feed frustrations in some people. Trying to understand deregulated plane fares or the role of video may trigger irrational responses in others. A job interview, a loan application, or a glaring deadline is probably making someone, somewhere dream of staying in bed for the next decade or so.

Unfortunately, there is no harmless way to practice juggling the bounding incorporeal balls of everyday life. Keeping up with the pace of modern living demands split-second timing and accuracy to boot; second guessing is a luxury for losers. One cannot drop one's family, job, or commitments painlessly. Hard decisions with long-range ramifications make it wise to stay on top of significant situations, and this is where juggling comes into its everyday best form. It steadies the mind and body in what may be the proper stance for juggling intangibles that we all must handle every day, whether we want to or not.

A juggler uses sharp timing, self-control, coordination, poise, physical and mental equilibrium, and well-integrated functioning of both halves of the brain to keep balls up, and these skills may help you keep many nonjuggling considerations clear in your life: Poise handles jobs. Good timing and self-control meet deadlines. Coordination helps keep you ready for change and mediates irrational responses. And both sides of the brain working in top form may be the best hope any of us has for keeping life in balance.

Part of the beauty of juggling is the crossover potential of a supposedly frivolous circus skill into spheres of being that arguably matter. Everything juggling teaches can give an individual better physical and intellectual control to deal with life's ups and downs, which are a lot like the paths of the balls: There are as many ways for life to unfold as there are tracks the balls may follow. Knowing when to wait and when to push is one key to success.

A juggler uses practiced skills to make the difficult look effortless, and though juggling will not make living stress-free, it can help you focus on making pressing challenges lighter, which may eventually guide you toward grace in whatever you do.

At the very least, juggling brings balance into your life. If your life is chaotic, learning to juggle teaches valuable skills of order. If your life is carefully ordered, juggling can offer you chance, excitement, and the likelihood of occasional, invigorating—but safe—chaos.

Who you are has everything to do with what juggling will ultimately do for you. Your body and brain will never be the same after you learn to JUST JUGGLE! And you can go even further with juggling if your heart is in it too.

CHAPTER
5

Emotional Benefits

Beyond the exertion and frustration of drops, and beyond the gymnastic mental balancing acts that are the fundamentals of learning to juggle, you stand at the heart of a juggling routine. Though misses will never be entirely eliminated and your brain will never feel perfectly equalized, there is a private place at the center of juggling where you may sense more than a rhythm of the balls, where you become the pulse of a juggling pattern, an active, alert, dynamic force holding chaos in check at the end of your fingertips.

Beyond Misses and into the Flow

Your space at the core of a rain of objects may be surprisingly calm. There, after seemingly endless misses, personal power that had been short-circuited will be able to course freely. Bending and stopping will become only infrequent distractions to motion and concentration.

And when the balls move with constancy under your control and you need to move very little, you may experience the distilled essence of juggling: A complex exercise may be performed subconsciously at sophisticated levels of attainment. When thought once pointed at how-to juggle can be blunted and dispersed by the release of pressure into the juggling act, a feat that had at first seemed like incomprehensible confusion may become second nature to you.

Think back again to riding that first two-wheeler. Sometime after that magical flash, bike riding became automatic. Driving a car, playing sports, tying your shoelaces, brushing your teeth, or signing your name involve coordination of complicated skills, but once most people have learned to do these things, they rarely, if ever, think about them or are in any way restricted by concern about their intricacy.

A similar learning pattern holds true for juggling. Once your body is practiced and your mind's eye is focused on a clear visual image, thinking too much about juggling may prevent you from doing it well. Our brains need time to process thoughts, but juggling happens faster—at the speed of instinctual reaction, where a juggler must learn to trust feelings refined by familiarity. Overt concern about movements that need to be fluidly sensed can make them come out choppy, and though it may help you learn to juggle by clipping your moves at first to establish forms clearly in your body and mind, a self-possessed juggling pattern needs to be felt more than reasoned out. Perceiving juggling's equipoise may be more useful than wondering where the next ball is coming from. And if you are open to them, juggling's symmetrical forms may relax you in less time than it might take to conjure up ideas of how good it would feel to be loose.

Relaxation

The certainty of a confidently directed pattern can soothe your mind, calm your nerves, and diminish anxiety. As you juggle, your breath evens and your eyes focus sharply, beaming like headlights peering into another dimension. Relaxed contentment warms your senses as your body moves at its own sleekest pace, coursing so concisely that it seems hardly in motion at all. Where once you had to think about each part of every juggling direction just to learn what moves felt like, everything runs more easily after you are comfortable with them. Your mind, freed in new open territory, may even feel dissociated from your body—and perhaps you will discern that there might be something else out there, something beyond body, beyond mind, something further beyond juggling. Like a tennis player who does not think to step right, step left, lift arm, swing, but responds with integrity to track and stroke a shot, you, too, can detect and dance to the private music of the spheres.

Music of Juggling

"Slap, slap, slap," the balls gently sound in meter against your competent palms as your breath rises and falls in cadence with the beat. With your quick hands to guide them,

WHY JUGGLE?

the props have a careful, reliable life of their own. This life, the tempo of the balls, is a hybrid between physical law and your body rhythms. If you wish, you may move extra-quickly, flinging balls rapidly with energy to burn. Or you may drift for a moment in a languorous, floating void outside of commonplace reality. At any tempo, you can improvise your own mesmeric tune against a

variable percussive backbeat of balls slapping skin, as current smooths through your neck and shoulders, down your arms and through your hands to push the balls, catch them, push, catch, and so on.

Once you become attuned to a well-defined task such as juggling, you may become totally occupied by it. The music of juggling can help you feel centered and engaged in the here and now. And focusing your energy may help clarify purposefulness. There is a secure sense of certitude to juggling, no loose ends, no questions, just clearly outlined objectives, heightened senses, and enhanced perceptions, which you create with your relaxed, clearly conscious mind. This is a considerably more melodic tune than the blare of widely used consciousness-altering techniques involving lids, ludes, liquor, anger, greed, or ego powertrips, which only create dependency and block the flow they were brought in to unjam.

Meditation and Transformation

The meditative potentials of juggling are interesting and wide open. After you can perform a repetitive task with feeling instead of thought, your conscious mind, once occupied by learning, may well be primed by accomplishment, ready and open to new challenges. Once you have established your capability, you may feel curiously drawn to expand on your newfound talents to press on toward synthesis of more information into fresh forms for making other dreams come true.

Juggling has the ability to transform you. Balls, rings, and clubs do nothing on their own. You handle them, and the interaction expands your senses to incorporate a new world. Juggling can be a relatively quick, enjoyable, safe, less stressful and more accessible way—beating out fasting, feasting, marathon running, or megavitamin therapy, to name a few popular others—to reach a place where pieces of life fit together and coexist in a private vision of peace, however briefly, while the balls are in the air. This may be juggling's version of spiritual clarity, even though the sport does not call for moral or religious fanaticism to master. It does, however, call for commitment, attentiveness, and sensitivity, traits which can do as much to calm a fuming, losing Little League coach as they can to elevate a guru-in-training. Juggling takes you to spiritual places only if that is where you want to go. For many people, though, mastering gravity may make it seem natural to lighten up altogether. Some will rise toward higher accomplishments of mind, body, and spirit.

People do, after all, need to get high somehow. Everyone needs release, if only occasionally, or if only for a moment—though not everyone admits it. Music provides it sometimes. Marijuana used to. Masturbation is always a strong comer, but a lonely finisher. Exercise works. And whole foods can help you do it—if you take care to taste them—if you can grow or find them.

The world can be a deadening place. Overcoming epidemic inertia seems to be the challenge of life in a complex culture where the rate of continuous change quickens all the time. Frontiers of knowledge multiply exponentially over months or weeks, rather than over lifetimes, leaving only fragments of yesterday's values intact. Economies falter, affecting millions of people, nations squabble and threaten each other, and people fail to treat each other with respect or with even a hint of compassion. It is easy to feel freaked out. And it is easy to see why so many people lean on crutches built of uppers and downers, sugar, spice, Scotch, Bourbon or beer, religious ecstasy, dollars or power brokering in the material world to try to feel good about themselves. But after getting high on artificial stimula-

tion, be it cocaine, caffeine, or cable TV, you come down hard and usually deeper into whatever rut you were in before, farther into whatever hole you tried to climb out of.

Yet, once you have been *high,* it is a tantalizing place to want to go back to, say on a more permanent basis. The only things that block your way are the limits of your body and imagination. But smack, snacks, smokes, gold, or anything you unilaterally take from the world will not get you out of or into those for very long.

Guess what can?

The more you juggle, the more you may become aware of your experience of freedom in a heightened state of consciousness. This liberty can give you a context for musings on what may be keeping you from juggling all the aspects of your life as neatly as you rotate the balls. Complaints, or negative emotions, and bad habits may be suddenly approachable with a new whole body, mind, and spirit that are yours to work with. And since juggling energy goes into the juggling—into the here and now, into keeping the balls in the air, not into being mad (as in angry *or* crazy), being tired, bored, petty, taken advantage of, late with the rent, a boss, a wife, a husband, a child, mature, poor, rich, or even in love—outside of these self-limiting, self-imposed handicaps and boundaries defining how we should be is who each of us is. Jugglers, like sky divers, yogis twisted into pretzel shapes, downhill ski racers, dancers, and musicians demonstrate that an effective way to get down to the soul of a particular reality is to prepare yourself, then let yourself go beyond restrictive thoughts and worries by trusting feelings and instincts.

Juggling teaches nothing if not how to let go fast. The crazy daily bombardment of rapidly changing knowledge, technology, and fashion knocks many of us out. Some are crushed and ground under in the excited movement to stay on top of things. Even an accomplished fool may offer something valuable once in a while. Flexibility, adaptability, and resiliency are qualities necessary for survival. If you cannot move along with a fast-moving scene, you may be in for a bumpy ride trying to hold onto yesterday's unyielding, outmoded values.

Fun

Juggling might be perceived as serious stuff if it were not so much fun to do. Flinging balls up and catching or missing them, attempting to promote continual flow, is pleasingly enjoyable in a slapstick comedy sort of way. It may seem as apparently senseless as the pie-in-the-face game, but both are pure release on a rarefield, instantaneously gratified level. Juggling may help you discover that playing by yourself, getting stronger, and increasing skills for coping with life's challenges can feel good. Working harmoniously in concert with a juggling plan, your awareness of pleasure may grow with all your blooming skills, and you may find a happy feeling of accomplishment inside you, of completion, and of satisfaction, however temporary.

Enhanced Awareness of Pleasure

When you juggle, with your feet planted, eyes focused straight ahead, and hands barely moving you perch in time—controlling your space, replenishing yourself by getting in touch with your innermost energies to sense as much as you can of your most joyful self. Increased awareness of gladness rounds out character—making it easier for a person to adapt, to imagine, to create and flow with the necessity of changing.

By playing with plastic clubs, or wooden rings, or rubber balls juggling lets you relax, clear out the day, clear your mind, add rhythm to your life, reduce tension, balance conflicting pressures, and equalize your brain halves and body parts. Juggling provides needed release and welcome comic relief from a too-serious and too-often tragic world. By mastering gravity a juggler possesses a moment of levity, and how many of us can afford to pass up a chance to make life feel lighter than it did before? And at considerable savings over therapy, worship, or drug addiction.

The line starts here. JUST JUGGLE!

CHAPTER
6

Other Benefits

Juggling is an ancient physical activity that falls into a hazy category somewhere between art and sport. It is a complex discipline that calls for concentration, coordination, and balance, which makes the process of learning to juggle unnatural (for many people), time-consuming (for most people), and at least occasionally frustrating for everyone. For example, everybody drops whatever they are trying to juggle many times before achieving any degree of consistency. Failure to reach any goal, however temporary the setback, may be unpleasantly disheartening. One may be sorely tempted to chuck the whole project and go back to watching TV, but for those who keep it up, juggling has proven over centuries that it has more to offer than voyeuristic diversion.

Fortitude

Desire to succeed and practiced movement toward a goal are the cornerstones of any achievement, juggling included. Ambition happily generates enthusiasm which can keep you going through rough spots of a learning process, and self-control helps you repeat again and again whatever motions are necessary for smooth mastery of juggling technique. The fortitude you demonstrate by sharp attentiveness to confirming control of evolving juggling patterns means that you have the right stuff needed to be a juggler. And these traits may help you do other things that you want to do.

Alert Body—Calm Mind

But even with the utmost concentration, everyone misses a lot at the beginning. Mistakes may cloud the light of learning, and small insecurities can grow into tension and worry that can destroy the all-important rhythm that you have struggled against gravity to set. With this in mind, it is fundamental to remember to relax while practicing; intent needs to be focused on juggling, but your reflexes must stay limber to continually react to each movement through many repetitions that you may have to throw before coming close to feeling what it is like to juggle.

Patience

Without a foundation in basic repetitive moves which are indispensable to good juggling technique, you may be able to learn to do simple object manipulations (such as a three-ball cascade), but unable to progress further along to higher juggling development which calls for more sophisticated skills and disciplines. Learning to juggle takes time that cannot be rushed. Drops take time to pick up—sometimes just to locate!—and impatient frustration is behind many complaints about the difficulty of learning to juggle.

It is impossible to overstate that blocked-up, intolerant students make lousy jugglers. Equilibrium is essential to good juggling. Without it, even the simplest routine gets far out of hand in no time at all. Tension and trying to practice juggling in an agitated mood make concentration difficult and juggling an all but insurmountable task, but stability comes hard to many people in a fast-changing society where yesterday's values are old and may be dangerous.

Calm, patient practice is the key. Juggling, like any goal, happens in time. Toleration and persistence can help direct and balance your mind and body. Free from anxiety about wild success or dismal failure, your determination to be as simply conscious as you can be, can make it all come together in ways that all the nervous worry in the world will never faintly approximate. After a drop, all you need to do is pick up the balls and start throwing again. Success will be yours if you keep going, though precisely how long it will take a student to catch on is hard to predict. Endurance and perseverance may be some of juggling's finer lessons. With these qualities, you may become increasingly attuned to your senses and burgeoning facilities for enhanced sight, touch, and hearing as they help promote a more perceptive, imaginative, creative, accurate, and balanced outlook toward whatever you encounter along the way.

Flexibility

Sometimes it seems as if mass trends in design, taste, and expectations are passing for stability. Television, fast foods, fad diets, reliance upon miraculous chemistry or magazine subscriptions, instead of upon healthy day-by-day practices, promote the fallacy that there is a right way and a wrong way to perceive. Juggling would be a great relief from stagnant viewpoints if it only offered an individual change of pace.

Take three rubber balls and throw them up in the air. Watch them bounce madly as they touch the ground. Try it again and again. You will probably notice that each time a ball lands it bounces differently; no matter how much care you take to make every throw the same, results always vary at least slightly. Changing patterns rely on many factors, including the height of the original throw, direction, landing spots, and obstacles. There is no single correct way for the balls to bounce.

A right–wrong-thinking individual courts disappointment and frustration in presuming that the balls are supposed to do one thing or another. A rigid personality may be guided by expectations that can prevent floating along with the immediacy of a less than wholly predictable current. A more flexible, less contrived personality, however, may be able to ride out any wave, moving rapidly with equal facility in any tide without going under. In that supple state, one may adapt to any eventuality. Legitimate physical balance, boosted by juggling, cuts across boundaries separating thought from action, and may be applicable to other facets of life beyond object manipulation.

Sense of Humor

Feeling good may ultimately be the best reason for juggling. Juggling makes most people smile anyhow, so it is a bonus that smiling keeps you from tensing up, gritting your teeth, and blocking your inner and outer forces. I repeat, everyone drops, even the best pros. No good is accomplished by frustrations directed at yourself for what you may perceive as terminal clumsiness. Your fury can only feed your ego which may stand in the way of reaching many goals, from mastery of juggling to mastery of self. Indeed, feeling silly or gawky because of an initial lack of manipulative finesse is okay. Bungling up goes with the territory and getting over it is a character-building exercise. Juggling is a game. Once you are past your insecurities, you may be able to laugh and enjoy yourself. And if you can laugh at yourself while you are fumbling around trying to juggle, then from the start, you will benefit by how substantially juggling can improve a sense of humor.

Release

There is more to juggling than misses, though it may not seem so at first. On the other side of frustration is sweet release. Juggling gives you a chance to control your energies by becoming purely concise for a moment of flawless motion that may be as close as any of us will ever get to any perfection. And although tossing a competent three-ball cascade need not be a prelude to any greater juggling feats, a limitless vista of potential achievement spreads open before an ambitious juggler after the cascade. There is much more that can be done—many ways to do it and much pleasure to be found along whatever way you choose to follow.

You decide which way to go. You may allow your ego and your unyielding values, possibly your worst enemies, to tie you up, or you may defer to the learning process and let it take you as far as your desire and abilities are able to travel. Ego rears up to justify failure, but releasing the bonds entangling your mind allows you to experience the rich diversity of juggling. A juggler is a master of gravity who exists in a state of levity that may be as close as we can get to feeling light in spirit, and perhaps forever young. You may find that juggling is a lot more fun than feeling sorry for yourself.

Self-Reliance

New powers rest in your hands alone, and eventually juggling teaches how to be alone. It is recommended for getting away from it all, but not to feel lonely and out of touch because of it. JUST JUGGLE! And make believe each ball is an everyday matter that normally holds you down. Learn to control the balls and you will realize that learning something new can make even a lone existence easier to handle. You may get accustomed to being alone and find out that it feels okay. Then you may find that it feels great in your corner of control in a perplexing world.

When you juggle, you have a place in life—a private peaceful domain wherever you are, whoever is around. What makes this place special is that you may find yourself there and perhaps discover a sense of your uniqueness. Your sense of balance, equilibrium, and oneness, and other associated strengths shown by your increased sensitivity and purpose of mind are the bases of self-confidence that helps you know who you are. These are the traits that can help get you through rough spots—a blockage in an evolving juggling process, a divorce, or a broken leg.

Independence is becoming a survival skill. Learning to live alone, to function self-reliantly, and to feel secure enough in the fragments of one's values that are left by sweeping changes in the human information base may be the challenge of the eighties. To keep going, to ride out the changes beyond your control and keep sight of who you are while those in your periphery seem to be faithfully following trendy conditions that do nothing for you is ever becoming more crucial to affirming dignity. Being true to yourself, moving to the beat of the little juggler in your head, is a hard way to go, but it may be the only way to go and still maintain an individual vision. In style or out of it, no one cares as much about your life as you do. Without self-esteem you are not even on your own side. Anyone who asks for that kind of trouble must be crazier than a juggler.

In order to derive satisfaction from juggling, you need to reach inside yourself and feel good about what you find. With self-confidence and self-assurance that come from learning to juggle, you may find that you do not need a fur-upholstered toothbrush or designer jeans, do not need status or acceptance, do not need to align yourself with any restrictive moral, political, or philosophical viewpoint to feel secure. Because you learned to do something that you may have thought you could not do, because you learned something completely new and survived, you have every reason to feel safe and sound.

Dreams

Standing steadily on your own feet—juggling—you master gravity, if only for an instant. Your greater consciousness of details allows you to examine fine points of any large proposition. You know that by applying your newly expanded abilities, by breaking large challenges into smaller bits and following easy steps one by one you can learn to juggle anything, even nice or nagging responsibilities like a job, a family, taxes, illness, stress, and so on. If juggling is your destiny, you have taken control of it, and you are fine. Attuned to yourself, you have reached a new harmonious state of inner and outer balance. Your private universe consisting of you and the pattern is yours to create in whatever image pleases you, and you feel better because of it.

You really do have something to smile about when you JUST JUGGLE!

PART III

The Method

TYPICAL JUGGLING INSTRUCTIONS ARE AIMED TOWARD PERFEC-tion of technique for performing. This book is tailored more flexibly toward whatever your individual needs are: Fun, exercise, relaxation, or dreaming. It stresses that missing is okay; and further, that if you keep working on accomplishing one-step-at-a-time, you will progress at your own pace. If there is perfection to be found, you will find it in the process of seeking release.

You may have noticed a little juggler appearing in the top-right corner of the right-hand pages of this book. Each drawing is slightly different from the one before or after it since each pose represents a highlight of a three-ball cascade juggling sequence. This may be seen by closing this book and grasping the top-right corner of the first page and the top-left corner of the last page between your right thumb and forefinger, and drawing your thumb across the edges of all the pages in between to make them flip in rapid sequence.

Keep your eyes on the little juggler. By flipping front to back, the individual drawings merge into an animated view of a dominant right-hand version of a three-ball cascade. (Lefties might prefer to start off with two balls in their left hands rather than in their right hands. But some may have trouble accomplishing a right-handed flip. In this case, I recommend practice with your right hand. Get with it. How can you expect to juggle with a hand that cannot flip the pages of a book?) With the flip sequence you can see what a three-ball cascade looks like altogether, and then look at single frames which neatly break the complex-looking juggling pattern into easily distinguishable visual pieces. The little juggler is your patient private instructor who is willing to go through every aspect of the routine with you as quickly or as slowly as you like, as many times as you want.

Never hesitate to flip through the animated sequence one more time. Become familiar with it. Flip at different speeds to catch every nuance. Memorize the image. Get to know what a cascade pattern looks like. Notice the relative and exact positions of the little juggler's arms, hands, eyes, and the juggling balls through any part of a three-ball cascade. If a step in your practice session hangs you up, simply isolate the corresponding spot in the flip sequence and study it backwards and forwards until you understand what you have been doing wrong, and correct it. No other juggling manual can duplicate the pin-point visual accuracy of this teaching method, which makes the quantum leap from reading a book to actually juggling a natural and easy progression for you to make.

To better "read" the animated sequence, always flip through about ten extra pages before the start of the frames you want to see. A lead-in to the flip will give you a chance to settle your grip and prefocus your vision for smoother flipping. Or try working with a partner (especially urged for clumsy lefties), so one can flip while the other juggles. Learn to see juggling in your mind; then, teaching it to your body will be easy.

Additional illustrations on coming pages represent a progression of juggling exercises from the patterns that you may want to know before you attempt the cascade to the more advanced patterns you may wish to pursue afterward. Don't be afraid to make another throw. By following all the coming steps for getting ready to juggle and by using the handy flip-book sequence, you can learn to do a three-ball cascade and other juggling cycles.

The cycle diagrams throughout the following chapters were designed to show the perspective you will have of your hands and the view you will have of balls in the air. While you are juggling, you will only be able to look at one of the angles (balls recommended), but the illustrations are meant to help you see ways to do more or less advanced juggling patterns, which you will be able to combine and interweave creatively with the cascade in your own imaginative designs. Looking back will make it all look easy, but every step, even the simplest one, has a purpose in clarifying the whole picture, as well as its own purpose, as an exercise. Please do them all. Repetitiousness, trysts with tedium, and coming to grips with misses are part of this plan, as are satisfaction, elation, and release. It all depends on how well you learn to chuck up and catch it.

JUST JUGGLE! On balance, everything will be okay.

CHAPTER
7

Goals

Learning a Three-Ball Cascade

The stated goal of this book is to teach the three-ball cascade pattern, which is a basis for all forms of juggling. To many people who do not know it, even such a simple pattern seems to be overwhelmingly complex. And yet some juggling students swiftly grasp the cascade and then eagerly move ahead into other juggling realms. Others will sense the opportunity the cascade presents for unifying consciousness and be content to work the pattern over and over again, throwing wider, higher, lower, or faster arcs for weeks, months or longer. What these approaches share is that juggling is possible at varying stages of difficulty, and that the choices that open before you once you can do the cascade are virtually limitless. You can enjoy making juggling as fundamental or complex as you wish.

Coping with Continual Change

All juggling depends on learning to cope with continual change, but intellectual posturing and theoretical mumbo-jumbo dim in consequence when the balls are in the air and the real forces at work are your integrity versus gravity. It takes preparation and attentiveness to master gravity, and if you try to do a three-ball cascade all at once in a rush, the contest may hardly seem a fair match. By breaking juggling down though, and considering one step at a time, each level may be given distinct attention until commanded fluently. If the next rung is difficult to grasp, the last step you were solidly on will hold you steadily so that you can maintain a sense of rhythmic balance that will eventually put you on top of a juggling routine.

This one-step-at-a-time teaching method will go through all the basics of learning the three-ball cascade, from where to stand and what to juggle to which hand does what and how, precisely, it all gets put together into juggling. Bits of information will acquaint your mind with the ideas, your body with the moves and your heart with the ambience of juggling so that slowly, with practice, juggling will become as hard for you to forget as how to shuffle a deck of cards. And continual change will be as easy for you to handle as a small rubber ball.

Just Juggling

Sooner or later there will be a moment when you *get* juggling for the first time. Suddenly, the balls may feel as if they are coming out of nowhere, as if they are moving by themselves, and you will no longer have to visualize the cascade pattern. You will feel it and know it as if it had existed in your mind all along, waiting for you to discover it. At that moment, you may have utterly defocused on yourself and your earthly cares, but your absorption with juggling will be complete, your movements alert, and  your mind relaxed at the same time. Your reflexes, your hands and eyes will be intent, centered, and responsive to constantly shifting information cues. Once you have become sensitive enough to read them, the moves can tell you everything you need to know. Once you are beyond this point, you will never forget the cascade pattern.

Combined enhancement of physical, rational, and intuitive sensitivity is more than a bonus of juggling: It is a platform for survival when coping with persistent variability in the world and in your head. If an advanced juggling pattern goes astray, you can always return to a fundamental cascade to regain your equilibrium before proceeding. Likewise, if you or your values fail—if your sense of time, place, or yourself disappears deep within one of life's tricky juggling sequences thrown indiscreetly out of control—the fundamentals of the cascade, concentration, patience, and a sense of rhythm may be the very factors that prevent you from losing your balls. In the midst of upheaval, if you can return to the self-reliant, fluid center of a path of least resistance, you may find that the heart of juggling will always be how you, a juggler, relate to changes in people, your planet, and yourself. Keen senses and selfless perceptions may even help salvage human decency and compassion when so many of our people are ever more remotely complex and numbly disinterested to boot.

Juggling may be new to you, but it has all been done before.

It simply requires that you rethink the order you give to things. Use the information that is available in these words and pictures, in your hands and eyes. Only specific hard juggling data count; nothing based on love, lust, rage, or paranoia will do. It can be wondrous to behold how layers of questionable responsibility in the material world peel away with rejection of such self-indulgent fancies.

If you let yourself go, the focused purpose and simple directness of juggling three balls may transport you to a parallel universe where you can soar alongside this world and its dissonant, cacophonous bleating will not distract your impeccable private rhythm. Keep juggling and you may become more pumped up with a rare clarity of vision which, if allowed to run its course, can penetrate far beyond the focal point of a pliant habit and core down to the soul of a juggler. At the center, you are, as you juggle, graceful or wasteful, pushy, mushy or sharp. Just juggling can give you all the latest information on efficiently using space, energy, motion, and time, and it may show who you are right now.

In the quest to cope with continual change, you may get a grip on yourself if you JUST JUGGLE!

CHAPTER 8

Equipment

Rolled-up socks, vegetables, fruits, or eggs (wisely, hard-boiled for beginners) are among household articles that may serve as convenient juggling props. Props are vehicles for transformation, for inventing new ways of experiencing familiar items. Like most valuable toys, the important things they can do are tap physical and intellectual resources, help unlock the imagination and shift creativity into drive. The props are less important than the possibility for growth they represent. Rocks, clocks, or woks can be juggled, although for learning the sport, the size, weight, and balance of specialized juggling equipment may make professional implements easier to handle.

Several firms in the United States and throughout the world produce juggling apparatus, much of which is mainly available through mail order (see propmakers list in chapter sixteen). Magic and novelty shops are usually the only retail outlets to stock specific juggling gear. Some jugglers make their own props, turning rings out of wood or plastic, and clubs out of scrub brushes or broom handles, but the mainstay of juggling is the rubber ball and these may be purchased ready-made from a wide variety of sources.

Juggling Balls

Several propmakers sell rubber balls, either specially made juggling balls which are designed for balance, density, bounce, and resiliency, or simply lacrosse balls, which share the right properties. Any rubber ball of two to three inches in diameter, weighing between four and six ounces, will probably make a good juggling ball. The best pro balls come with smooth, glossy finishes in bright colors that reflect light well to be easily "read" by an audience. But a good quality, small, four-ounce ball, whether glossy or not, is the prop I recommend for beginners. Some of these are available with ribbed surfaces—for traction, I suppose—which may at least psychologically give you a better grip on juggling at early stages of practice.

A set of four pro balls costs less than dinner at a good restaurant (under twenty dollars), and is the only equipment you need for virtually countless hours of juggling. If your tastes run more to fast foods, sponge rubber balls at less than one dollar each may be found in toy shops, and are okay to use if they have any bounce. Hollow rubber balls are too light for serious juggling. And tennis balls, which teasingly come packed in sets of three, are hard to resist juggling while waiting for a court (a great way to meet people), but they are light too—and actually lousy for juggling. Baseballs and billiard balls are not made of rubber. They do not bounce well and can hurt you, although they come in good sizes and weights for juggling. Golfballs, softballs, basketballs, or bowling balls may be juggled with varying degrees of ease, if you so desire.

Beanbags

Next in popularity as a prop for beginners to work with may be the beanbag. They share with balls the handy quality that they may be caught by grabbing any of their surfaces from any direction. Additionally, beanbags do not bounce, and thus do not have to be chased very far when they are misthrown. Although this may be considered an advantage in some circles, chapter nine suggests ways to neutralize the bounce in good rubber balls until you want it back, eliminating the need for an intermediate prop like a beanbag. However, if all you want to do is to maintain the best grip you can on learning the cascade, the bags, which are easy to make or purchase, can be substituted for balls in all but bouncing patterns, and may work well for you.

Produce, Soup Bones, and Canned Goods

Numerous varieties of produce may serve as juggling props. Thick-skinned navel oranges and grapefruits can be good props if you can find samples in the right size and weight range. Citrus fruits will leave your hands smelling nicer than rubber balls and withstand the rigors of juggling fairly well; if you do not miss too many times, they may still be edible when you finish practicing.

Apples do not fare so well. They bruise easily when dropped and are quick to become mushy, wet, slippery, and impractical for juggling. But they are made to order for a popular juggler's trick of biting in mid-juggle (an unpeeled orange would taste dreadful), and so will always have a place in a sure-handed pro's propbox.

Acorn squashes, small cabbages, avocados, mangos, and potatoes are a few other organic items that make a produce market a juggler's dream. Already, here and there, I have seen pomegranates, pears, and peppers popping into the air in supermarkets as jugglers indulged in an irresistible urge. And when juggling really catches on, produce aisles might begin to look like schools for jugglers working out new patterns in front of different bins. What with much of today's supermarket produce grown carefully for traveling far to distant markets, instead of for outmoded qualities such as texture and taste, then picked long before ripeness to stay reliably hard for shipping, juggling some foods may actually be more palatable than eating them. Other supermarket sections yield marrow bones and canned goods which may also be adaptable for juggling.

Rings, Clubs, Cigar Boxes, and Other Standards

Rings, clubs, cigar boxes, and fire torches are other items available from propmakers at prices ranging from twenty dollars and up for a set of three twelve-inch plastic rings or twenty-inch clubs to thirty dollars and up for a set of three good fire torches (you don't want to hear about bad fire torches!).

Rings (also called hoops) are nowadays molded from unbreakable plastics and weigh about the same as juggling balls. Lighter-weight rings are less tiresome for beginners to handle, but heavier hoops are more stable in flight, for greater control. Rings are showy and excellent to juggle for numbers. The world's record for cascading balls is nine, but the world's record for juggling rings

is eleven. Many jugglers believe that rings are easier to juggle than balls or clubs.

Clubs may be more difficult to juggle than balls or rings. Since a club is linear rather than circular or spherical, one must be *flipped* precisely in space and time, in order to turn over in the air, be catachable by its handle, and thus positioned securely in an unfolding juggling pattern.

Clubmakers are among the most creative of propmakers. Experimental use of ever lighter-weight plastics and inexpensive molded one-piece forms, short or long handles, stubby or slim knobs and bodies, and stock or custom-painted finishes are available. Choosing a club may be a formidable chore, but there is a certain majesty to a club spinning

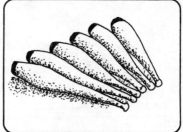

through the sky, which may entice you into clug juggling. Moreover, a lightweight club with a long handle will give you the most airtime and a relatively large target to grab without dislocating your arms. And then your style and preferences will determine the type of clubs you like to juggle.

Reinforced wooden cigar boxes, similar to the ones W. C. Fields flipped and manipulated (differently from ball juggling), at around twenty-five dollars per set of three are often used by jugglers. And many pros really use fire torches in their acts. These are generally aluminum rods with asbestos or other flammable wicks that may be soaked in lighter fluid and lit without being burnt up. Flame torches are not advised for novices. But if nothing else will light your fire, remember not to practice under a smoke alarm or sprinkler system.

Juggling sharp-bladed instruments always holds the fascination of both an audience and a juggler. Knives, long machetes, axes, sickles, and hatchets need to be well-balanced to cut well, and their evenly distributed weights make them good props in some respects. Personally, I think you have to be crazy to juggle things that can kill you, but there are those who insist. So I must state unequivocally that juggling sharp instruments is not advocated for anyone. If you must try it, please tape all blades and wear a crash helmet to protect your head, for whatever it may be worth.

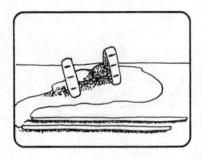 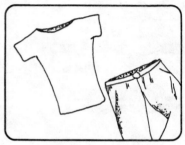

Miscellaneous Props and Attire

There are a few more juggling props that you may have seen but cannot name. The diablo (about ten dollars and up for the ones imported from China) is an hourglass-shaped Oriental whistling top that is spun on a string between two handsticks. Devil stick sets comprise three sticks, two thin handsticks and a tapered-toward-the-middle devil stick that gets batted back and forth through the air between both hands. Fire devil sticks, for pyros only, cost fifteen dollars and up. And plates for spinning on long dowels cost twenty dollars and up, and are often seen on stage, although they are, along with cigar boxes, devil sticks, and the diablo, beyond our concerns here. Most stores carrying the basic juggling props—balls, rings, clubs, and beanbags—will also stock at least a small line of more advanced gear. Clerks who know how to use the equipment are normally eager to demonstrate juggling devices, and some props come with brief instructions to help get you started.

Once you have gathered the props you will be using, it may help you to be comfortably dressed to juggle. Ease of move-

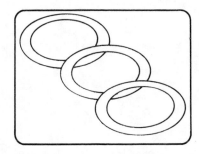

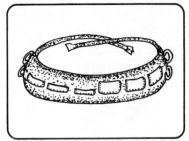

ment is important for a juggler. Performers wear glittery, tight, spangled outfits, which are fine for stagework, but for the needs of a solitary juggler, ordinary light cotton duds may be the best costume.

Juggling demands senses rooted in the here and now. Exercising in natural fiber clothing is suggested since man-made fabrics cannot absorb sweat. Cottons let your skin breathe, and you may also appreciate their light weight and natural stretchiness.

The simplest dress seems to work best. Stick with T-shirts, baggy pants, shorts or jeans, sneakers or Chinese cotton shoes with thin rubber soles that let you feel the ground. Some jugglers wear special belts or capes to hold their props, and these may be useful if you do not mind rings and clubs clapping against your thighs or ribs. And an old silk top hat and a cane, if you can find them, are always classy and nice, impressive if you can do tricks with them, but by no means necessary trappings. Keep in mind that props, costumes, and accessories that overshadow the juggling or interfere with a juggling routine have nothing to do with learning to JUST JUGGLE!

CHAPTER
9

The Place

For beginners, where to juggle may be more important than what to juggle. Generally, anyplace with adequate lighting, indoors or outdoors, that provides enough room for a person to stand and stretch his or her arms in any direction is probably an alright juggling spot for an *experienced* juggler. A beginner, however, may fare better in a specially controlled environment with well-known reference points for orientation.

Picking Your Juggling Spot

Choosing a place that you can return to as many times as necessary to master the cascade and other basic patterns may be a good idea. You do not have to stay in one spot after you learn juggling fundamentals, but since recognized scenery tends to disappear into familiarity and be less distracting to you, a cordial location for practicing any new business or routines may subliminally help you keep your sight set on juggling.

I believe it is best to pick a place to learn the three-ball cascade indoors. Physical limits that walls and a ceiling impose on a juggler are desirable disciplines for making concise throws a practical necessity in this case. The precision demanded for learning to juggle within the snug restraints of a ten-by-twelve-foot room with an eight-foot ceiling will ground you in good juggling habits that you may particularly appreciate when you begin doing advanced stunts.

A room where you will disturb no one, and vice versa, is recommended. Jugglers need to be able to concentrate on reading their senses. Irate downstairs neighbors kept awake by your practicing on their ceiling, or curious well-meaning friends who just want to watch or talk about juggling would rate equally as disturbances. Happily, in your small, manageable environment, such intrusions may be anticipated and held in check by valuable forethought which may also help set your mind on the juggling.

Clearing Your Space

Before you begin to practice, it may also be necessary for you to take care of inanimate objects in your juggling room. For safety's sake, anything that a stray juggling ball might break—lamps, pictures, vases; become annoyingly entangled in—shoes, a ceiling fan, a box of kitty litter; or be temporarily or permanently lost because of flying out an open window, landing in a pot of soup or rolling under an immovable one-ton sofa bed— again!, might best be removed or eliminated from the immediate juggling environs. Indeed, there is only one important piece of furniture that belongs in a juggling practice room.

The sole piece of furniture that you may want to keep in your juggling place happens to be the heart of my special number-one-secret-up-the-sleeve-spectacular-surprise-trick for making learning to juggle easier than you ever imagined it might be. Yes, one common item can instantly relieve you of the primary source of distress and frustration that afflicts many student jugglers. The piece is a bed and the trick is this: Learn to juggle over a bed so you will not have to chase your drops very far. Any size bed will do, but a single bed may be best, unless you have extremely long arms to reach across a wider one.

Establishing Your Juggling Corner

Push your bed into a corner where there are preferably no windows or doors on the adjacent bare walls (which may serve your needs best if they are solid-colored, to give the balls a clear backdrop). You might want to tack a plain bed-sheet over distracting wallpaper. Ordinary bed clothes will neither interfere with juggling nor be damaged by it. But remove anything else from the bed, including all your friends, juggling equipment, old clothes, children, pets, or your lunch. This is *your* juggling corner. If you stand alongside the bed and face the niche when you practice jug-

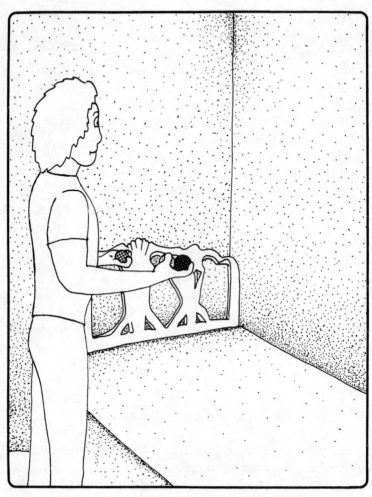

Clear your space. This is your juggling corner.

THE METHOD

gling, the walls will usually block the horizontal flight of wide throws, the ceiling will limit the height of your throws, and the bed will catch most (not all—you will be amazed at where misses may end up) of your drops. In your bed-corner, time normally spent hunched-over, retrieving drops—perhaps the most distracting part of learning to juggle—may be lavished on additional throws and  catches, which will get you juggling and out of your confining little room in the shortest span possible. There will be plenty of time for wild drops later, while you are learning difficult bits that cannot be practiced over a bed.

A standard American bed height works nicely for bolstering a juggler's shins. Beginners have a natural tendency to throw balls forward rather than up into the air. But if your legs are butting up against a bedframe, then you will not be able to follow after forward misthrows. Without the bed to block your way, you could run after these bad throws and perhaps even hold on to a retreating juggling pattern for a few throws longer. But misthrows have an utterly reliable way of multiplying upon themselves; eventually, they will trip you up. And it is, therefore, best to minimize their impact as much as possible. Between the bedframe obstructing your legs and the walls and ceiling impeding your bad throws, your cozy juggling corner is certain to keep even your least skilled efforts reasonably contained.

Failing to produce a corner bed on a frame for your juggling practices, your next best bet might be a bare mattress in a corner of the floor. But juggling over anything that can deaden drops without sliding around a room when you butt into it is worth trying. Bolted-down hotel beds may be good to juggle over. Waterbeds are okay, but you may need a truck to move one if it is not in a corner already. And the undulating motion of a liquid-filled bed might make you dizzy. You can count on lots of bending and straightening up, no matter what you juggle over, and with waves rolling in the bed and balls rising and floating on the swells, the waterbed route could be a mistake for you, unless you are a sailor. But its immobility would be a plus in any case.

It may be funny, for example, to watch a struggling juggler push a traditional bed on wheels around a room while trying to catch up with a going-out-of-control juggling routine, but it will be less fun—not much, really—to be that fussing juggler. Whatever you set yourself up over, the corner setting is the ideal. Perhaps the extra effort you put into rearranging furniture will give you added incentive to practice minutes longer at a stretch, or work harder right off the bat, because you already have time and energy invested in this juggling business before you have even picked up a juggling ball.

Alternate Settings

If no bedding whatsoever is available for your practice sessions, a corner placement over a thick shag rug or carpet, or over flat pillows, or a foam mat may work for you. Anything that will dampen the potential bounce of a missed juggling ball can be helpful. If you have a bathtub enclosed by three walls you might try filling the tub with water and practicing in the little alcove. Caution: Do not juggle beanbags over water; you might get bean sprouts; use only balls that float.

Juggling is, of course, possible outdoors. But standing in the open air with no focal frame for perspective may make learning to keep the balls in a tightly controlled pattern difficult for beginners. Indoors, a plain, familiar backdrop makes sighting the balls in the air a relatively easy task, while there are usually many distractions outside.

If you must juggle outdoors, try to keep the balls in line and yourself from moving about maniacally by picking a practice spot just as you would indoors. Good places might be over thick grass facing a wall of a house or building, or over sand facing a tall fence. Beachgoing jugglers might suspend a blanket from two beach umbrellas for a glare-resistant backdrop. And truly ambitious seaside jugglers might even dig a thigh-deep hole in the sand

to stand in, so drops could land on the ground at hand level and you would barely have to flex to retrieve misses. At a calm beach, a lake, or pool, standing in shallow water to float misses might work nicely.

And indoors or out, handy jugglers might want to fashion a portable net for catching misses wherever they may occur. Simply salvage an old hula-hoop. Tape, staple, tie, or glue fish netting around the circumference of it. Cut a hole in the middle of the net that is big enough to fit around your waist. Stand in the hole. Slip on a pair of suspenders and clip them to the net. JUST JUGGLE! and the net will snag most of your drops. Or as a last resort for handling the challenge of misses, you might simply accept them, chase them, and relish the exercise. The truly best place to juggle is probably standing over a solid hardwood floor in a bright, diffusely lit room with high ceilings, like a gymnasium.

Anyplace where you decide to learn to juggle, inside or out, must be readied. Remember to move furniture if you have to. Take pictures down from walls. Put clocks, radios, computers, and any other breakables in the next room, and make sure there are no prize petunias or video games nearby. Wherever you may be, the commitment you put into personalizing your juggling spot may help shorten the time you will need to learn the cascade and any other patterns you may be interested in.

Setting Yourself

When your room or outdoor spot is set up, prepared, and obstacle-free, begin to work on getting yourself the same way. You want to feel comfortable and open to appreciate this new juggling experience, so standing where you will juggle, with your feet flat on the floor and your spine straight, let your arms dangle. Feel your body becoming relaxed as you breathe deeply down into your lower abdomen without heaving your chest; your stomach should move in and out instead. After several deep breaths, close your eyes and yawn to restore a natural breathing rhythm. Feel the tension in your neck release.

When you are calm and breathing normally, with your dominant hand, pick up one of the three juggling balls you have set before you on the bed or wherever you are. Turn the ball over in your hand. Feel its roundness. Squeeze it softly, then harder; feel its density, its texture, its substance. Shake it as if you were gently rattling a die. Pass the ball to your other hand, and repeat your examination.

The first frame of the animation sequence on page one illustrates the proper way to hold three balls in the rest, or starting, position for a three-ball cascade—two balls are gripped in the dominant hand, one ball is cupped loosely in the other hand. Please pick up your three juggling balls. Hold them just as they are being held in the drawing. If you have already become familiar with the animated flip drawings in this book, and observed other jugglers, then you may know so well what juggling looks like that you can almost feel it. It may be easy for you to imagine that you are juggling.

Close your eyes. Relax. Breathe evenly, deeply into your abdomen. Visualize what it would be like to be juggling. Think of how it would look to you and how it would look to someone watching you. Imagine how the balls would feel against your hands, what your eyes would see and what tracking they would do. Think of what your juggling routine would sound like and how the rubber balls would smell. The place where juggling really happens is in you. Hold the full sensory image in your mind.

See, I told you it was easy to JUST JUGGLE!

CHAPTER
10

The Body

Once you have established your juggling spot, you will want
to learn to feel right in various juggling positions. Juggling
may eventually relax you deeply and transport you to new
dimensions of reality, but first you must learn to do it. To do
that, you may need to reach into the center of your being to
clear yourself of distractions and precisely coordinate your
energies toward the motion at hand. Composure, openness
and responsiveness will help you master yourself. All else
comes after that.

Teaching Yourself to be Prepared

A juggler's body is sensitized, alert and yet loose enough to respond instinctually while the mind stays clear and calm. You may be able to help yourself approach these conditions by stretching your body to limber up before you juggle. Warm-up exercises may help dissipate body tensions that can interfere with the smooth energy flow needed for juggling. And time wisely taken to relax yourself into balance between inner needs and outer environments may help free your mind of that important task while you are juggling. If, for reference, you can also imagine controlling a perfect point of equilibrium where you and the setting would vanish and all that could be seen would be the juggling, such an image may help you establish the clarity of focus needed to juggle. Privacy, warm-ups, and creating idealized visual images may help cue you in on a juggling groove that can be used to your advantage, since it will generally be impossible for you to juggle if your attention is diverted elsewhere. Suggested warm-ups are also particularly good for burning up disruptive excess gusto or for unsticking rusted parts of a disused body.

Use these mental and physical warm-ups at your own speed. After you do the routines several times, you may know the exercises and your needs well enough to do without this book for reference. But a partner may be helpful to you at this time to read the instructions slowly out loud at a pace that allows you to repeat each step as many times as you need to fully relax and center yourself before working on throwing and catching. Later, partners can switch places. These warm-ups take little time or space to accomplish. Remember them whenever you want to communicate with your bones, clear your brain, or concentrate on anything.

Warm-Ups

To begin, place your three juggling balls down on the bed in front of you. Stand with your knees slightly spread, your arms hanging loosely at your sides. Look around to acquaint yourself with the layout of your prepared juggling spot. When you feel centered, put your hands on your knees, bend your head upside down and flick it vigorously from side to side for ten seconds, as if you were shaking out wet hair.

Stand up straight. With your arms dangling, twist your shoulders from front to back, as far as you can, several times. Then, interlace your fingers behind your head, twist around a few more times and bend slowly forward, backward and each sideway at your waist. With your hands still behind your head, do six or more deep knee bends.

Stand up straight on one leg, shake your other leg, and wiggle the foot. Switch legs and repeat.

With both feet on the ground, look directly ahead at a wall. Keep your eyes open but do not concentrate on seeing anything in particular. Breathe deeply in and out. If your head and neck or any parts of your body that you have just worked on feel tight or uncomfortable, massage them by hand and patiently repeat any exercises you need to before continuing.

Take three long, deep breaths.

Put your hands on top of your shoulders and alternately swivel each shoulder by pointing your elbows as far forward and back as you can.

Put your arms in front of you at shoulder height and lace your fingers together so that your knuckles face you. Stretch your arms and push out slowly with your entwined hands.

Relax. Then repeat several times and shake your hands in the air to loosen your wrists.

Massage each of your arms from the shoulder down, working slowly over your elbows, forearms and wrists. Massage your hands and each finger. Flex your hands by alternately extending your fingers and clenching them into fists, and let your arms dangle at your sides.

Close your eyes. Breathe deeply, slowly in and out. Focus yourself by concentrating on how relaxed your feet feel, and let the tranquility spread up your legs, through your middle, and into your neck. You want your head, face, and eyes to feel rested, your mouth and jaw to feel tension-free. Breathe evenly. Go as slowly as you need to calm yourself.

When you feel stabilized, look at one of your juggling balls or at some other brightly colored object. Fix on the object without straining your eyes. Notice its color. Shut your eyes and keep the color in mind. Inhale, then exhale slowly and fully.

Open your eyes onto the object. The color may appear to be brighter than you had imagined it. Reposeful eyesight tends to see things more sharply than tired eyes, if only for a moment roughly equal to the time of rest. Unfortunately, you cannot guarantee keen eyesight by simply closing your eyes for a few seconds. It is difficult for the eyes to relax if the mind is not at peace; an agitated mind seeks restless imagery. Your ability to rest your eyes correlates to the calmness of your mind, and it may help you regulate your vision as well as serenity, each being important juggling factors.

You may be able to judge how relaxed your eyes are by cupping your hands over your closed eyes and trying to see perfect blackness; in the absence of light, pure blackness is what there is and what you should see. The more peaceful you feel, the more blackness you will see. Any bright colors or light flashes that may appear in your vision are works of imagination better saved for juggling. It may help you to remember the color by looking at something black before you close and cover your eyes. Or try thinking of five or six black items in a row, a black sock, a black shirt, a black suit, and so on. When solid black is all that you see, then your eyes and your mind are basically as calm as you want them to be for optimum juggling results.

Stretching your body to work out small kinks and resting your eyes to strengthen your sight should help you approach a personally vigorous and equilibrated foundation for learning to juggle. Make sure you feel comfortable doing any of the exercises. Teaching your body to remember these relaxed starting points may make it easier for you to get in touch with juggling every time you move into your juggling spot.

Rest Position

When you are stretched-out, warmed-up, calm, and well-settled in your juggling corner, the starting position for doing a three-ball cascade is simply this: Stand straight, with your feet spread comfortably at about shoulder-width. Let your upper arms dangle at your sides, but bend your elbows up at ninety-degree angles so that *if* you were holding juggling balls loosely in your upturned, cupped hands, the balls would stay put in front of you. You can check your position against the start of the flip sequence and the corner setting illustration on page seventy-eight. Then close your eyes while still in the rest position. Reach out with your arms, swing your shoulders, and twist around on your spot. Feel your body stretch through each movement, then return to rest position, and open your eyes. Re-place yourself back in your spot, using familiar reference points to secure your balance.

Pick up three juggling balls, two in whichever hand you prefer, and assume the rest position exactly as you see it in the illustrations. Hold your forearms equally high without squeezing the balls. If you have trouble holding two balls in one hand, you may need to get smaller balls. Hold your head straight and still, but not stiffly, focus your vision on a wall or whatever broad, plain surface is in front of you, then close your eyes and think of blackness. Feel the symmetry of your head squared to your shoulders, of your steady arms and hands. Make adjustments to your stance for balance. Good form makes you exercise the muscles you want to work. If you concentrate on sensing equilibrium in your pose, then your efforts will produce the results you aim for.

Moving Toward Balance

Think about your balanced stance from head to foot in the beginning. Learning to juggle involves numerous repetitions of many exercises, and the basic rest position is the balanced starting point for every rep. If you direct yourself deliberately toward good form for the foundation, then, when you become used to it, you will be able to settle into it without thinking at all. And your poised rest position will help smooth out everything that flows from it. It can help you feel where your body may be tight or straining, and it is the basis of your awareness of keeping your movements fluid, not jerky. Try always to return to the rest position after moving out of it, to rebalance yourself, and for reference to how far from equilibrium and your greatest potential for alert responsiveness your juggling may have taken you.

Once you feel secure in the rest position, force yourself to do a few more knee bends or waist twists, with corresponding returns to rest. If possible, check your stance in a large mirror to actually see the balance you have been striving for. Commend or correct yourself accordingly. Juggling in front of a mirror is a wonderful way to be sure if you are still smiling and to check your progress at any stage of learning. Be forewarned: Beginners may find the sudden sight of six balls in the air where only three were in hand a moment before to be alarming. But if mirrors do not dizzily distract you or otherwise cause you to laugh too hard to juggle, you may want to practice watching your reflected image instead of the real action to see if you can shift yourself into exquisite balance while you juggle!

If you start from your rest stance, from a centered, ready figure, and return to your rest position whenever you miss or experience a break in the juggling action, then you will always be able to renew your concentration. Later, the cascade pattern will serve a similar restful, balancing purpose *during* a juggling routine. The cascade is commonly the familiar pattern jugglers fall back on when other trickier business is getting out of hand; it is a moving "rest position" for experiments in advanced juggling work. But experiments may only be hopefully pursued from a solid foundation of knowledge. A well-thrown cascade pattern to fall back on while working out new stunts will eventually give you the same kind of security that the simple rest position will give you while you learn the cascade.

Feeling Right

When you think you have learned completely how to do any phase of juggling, when you are positive that you have a new motion or even the basic rest position down totally to habit, practice the motion or strike the pose ten more times to perfection. There is only one person you can cheat on this. Go ahead, do it again. Be conscious of teaching your body to remember how it feels when its inclinations are centered, and also remember that inflexibility is never correct. Feel right with your best notion of

good form and gain confidence from it. Seek your most comfortable margins of mobility and control, your personal cloud within which competent juggling can occur. Juggling may ultimately be more valuable than good form, but exercising good form is the surest way to learn to juggle.

When you feel completely natural in rest position, stand on your juggling spot and hold your forearms up at waist level with your three juggling balls in your two hands. Inhale slowly. Take a deep breath in through your nose to fill yourself with air, then slowly exhale through your mouth. Feel the stability of your stance. Note the balls gripped loosely in your hands. Inhale once again. Feel composure spread in balance through your eyes, lungs, arms, wrists, hands and all your fingers. Exhale, quickly, if you must.

Put the balls down on the bed. You are ready to JUST JUGGLE!

CHAPTER
11

The Moves

Pick up one juggling ball in your dominant hand, and return to your rest position. Grip the ball loosely in your upturned, cupped hand, letting the ball rest in your palm. You may let your other hand drop to your side if you like, but keep the hand with the ball at waist level. Take time to relax, to center yourself within your body and within the space of your juggling spot.

One Ball in One Hand

When you feel calm and ready, lightly toss the ball straight up as high as your face, springing it off of the ridge at the base of your fingers so that your wrist and forearm move very little. Catch the ball in the same hand, without looking down at it or moving from your spot, if you can, and stop immediately.

If you managed a perfect throw, it would have risen from the thrusting base of your fingers, not from their tips, spreading the digits outward from the centered force of the push. Your wrist would have snapped slightly but not *broken,* and your forearm would have remained level at waist height to hold your hand in exact position to close back perfectly naturally around the descending ball.

Retake the rest position. Toss the ball straight up again, this time with an image of a good juggling throw in mind. Try to spring the ball firmly and catch it in the same hand without moving. Keep your eyes focused in front of you, on the highest point of the ball's flight, and practice throwing to exactly the same place with each toss of the ball. Try again and again until you can reliably pitch every ball smoothly to face height and catch each throw without looking at your hand.

Learn to sense where a ball will land by watching its peak. It may be physically possible for you to nod your head up and down like a yo-yo to follow a single ball with your eyes, but later, with more balls to contend with, there will be precious little time to focus anywhere but on the peaking flights of each one, without courting motion sickness or a sprained neck. It is less dizzying, less dangerous, and easier to learn the simple but necessary juggling skill of keeping one's eyes pointed upward and outward with a lone ball than with two or three. And if you throw to the same place every time, soon you will know where every toss will land. Consistently accurate tosses will become mandatory later on for doing complex juggling routines built on precision, and well-spent practices at this early stage can save time later by eliminating any future chance of your having to unlearn bad habits.

When you can make a one-ball throw and catch without thinking about it, make four more excellent tosses and grabs, and then switch over to your other hand. Practice with your weaker hand until you are competent at the same pattern with it too. (If you feel awkward, out of synch or out of control with weaker-hand throws, return to dominant-hand throws for a few tosses; when you feel completely loose and sharp with your stronger hand, switch right back over to your other one and practice with it some more—the dominant tempo may transfer to the other side.) When your right- and left-hand throws are steadily rising face high, and you are catching all your tosses routinely without looking at your hands, stop.

One Ball in Two Hands

Compose yourself in the rest position with the same single ball in your dominant hand. Take three deep breaths to center yourself. Remember to focus on the high points.

Spring the ball up into the air so that it traces an inverted V in space, peaking in front of your face, before landing in your other hand. Spring it back the same way, making sure it moves only vertically and horizontally at a consistent depth.

Practice for a few minutes, making each distinct throw from waist height. Try to keep your hands in rest position for catches too. Then toss a throw from your dominant hand, and without gripping it in your other hand to make a conclusive catch, snag the ball lightly instead, and spring it immediately up and back across to your dominant hand. Your final catch should then complete an invisible two-dimensional bow tie design traced in the air by the trail of the ball from hand to hand and back again.

Look at figure one. Study it and try to duplicate the illustrated hand-and-ball positions. Try to keep the ball moving smoothly along a bow tie outline drawn in your mind. Do not tightly clutch the ball until the last catch of any sequence. Direct it in motion, by shoveling under your first throw at the lowest

Figure 1. ONE-BALL-TWO-HANDS PATTERN. (1) Rest; (2) right throws; (3) peaking at head height; (4) left catches;

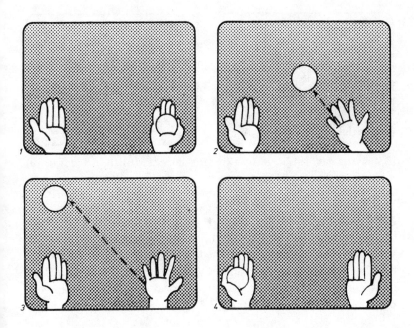

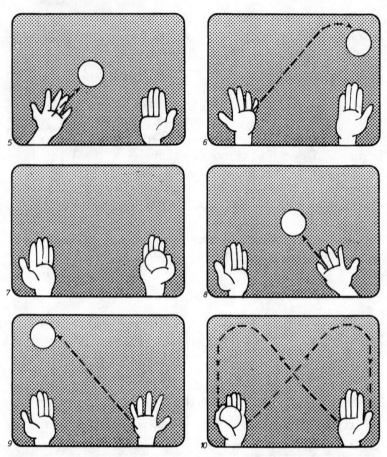

(5) left throws; (6) peaking; (7) right catches; (8) right throws; (9) peaking; (10) left catches.

point of its path on the other side of the bow tie, and when the momentum of the scooping motion *begins* to carry your weaker hand up the lower inside of the bow tie toward its middle, propel the ball up into another face-high arc. The next catch may then be shoveled in at the opposite lowest point of the bow tie and scooped up toward the middle, to be sprung for another throw up and across to another shoveling catch and throw, and so on, for as long as you want.

The two-dimensional bow tie outline is the fundamental route of a three-ball cascade, so it may be wise to work through this one-ball-in-two-hands exercise many times, even though it is relatively simple. Try not to spin the ball off your fingertips or out of your palm, but rather spring it up from the ridge at the base of your fingers. (Keeping the ball under your complete control will be easiest if it has no spin of its own to interfere with your direction. Mark lines on the ball with a pen, if you cannot easily see if it is rotating in flight.)

Take care to keep throws equally high and wide at a consistent depth, focus on the peaks, and keep your hands down near waist level. Your arms may ride up a few inches to make throws, but they need not move up to catch a ball. Always wait patiently for the ball to come down; you may be able to master gravity eventually, but you will never make it go away. Later on, when you have no spare time for extra moves in the midst of a cascading routine, you may appreciate every moment you spent concentrating on this easy stuff.

When you can throw consistent two-dimensional bow ties with one ball in two hands, starting with either hand, toss five more measured circuits of ten consecutive throws each, and rest. The next phase may be more challenging.

Alternating One Throws

Pick up another ball so that you have one ball in each hand in rest position. See, you are making progress.

Now, concentrate. Breathe. When you feel centered, start by springing the first ball straight up out of your dominant hand to face height, exactly as you did the first one-ball-in-one-hand exercise in this chapter. When that ball *begins* to come back down into the same hand, pitch the second ball up from your other hand, in parallel with the falling ball. Then, as the second ball approaches its peak, catch the first ball in the hand that threw it. Then grab the second ball with the hand that threw it.

Alternating throws and catches with one ball in each hand is not juggling, but if you run enough of them together, it looks neat. And even the basic two-throw may strengthen skills you need for juggling; this practice can help develop needed peripheral vision—if you concentrate on focusing on a point between the two peaks—and teach important timing for tossing one ball up every time another ball passes its highest point in the air.

Continuously working your hands separately in equivalent staggered rhythms is what much of juggling is all about. Work toward making your throws straight, by springing the balls up, not rolling them off your fingertips. And wait patiently for the first throw to pass its highest point before you launch the next toss. Then wait for that throw to start coming down before respringing the first ball, and so on.

Focus on a point between the peaks: Alternating one throws may strain your eyesight or your mind if you try to do otherwise. This is fairly complex business. Your eyes may feel simultaneously drawn in many different directions that you cannot possibly follow. Work on making consistent throws so that you only have to consider the high spots at the edges of your vision. Remember that it is not your eyes that make catches—if your throws are accurate, your timing sharp and your hands sensitive, catches will take care of themselves.

Practice alternating throws and catches until your tosses are crisply consistent and your grabs clean while your head is

steady. Make sure you feel comfortable throwing and catching in alternating rhythm by combining ten throws — five from each hand — without a break in between. Repeat the ten-throw pattern five times without missing before moving ahead.

Two Balls in Two Hands

Return to rest position with one ball in each hand. Breathe deeply three times. When you feel relaxed, spring the ball up from your stronger hand. You want it to cross in front of your face as it approaches the opposite top point of a bow tie pattern on its way to your other hand, but when the ball begins its descent from the highest point of its flight, spring the second ball up *under* it, to trace out the other top side of the bow tie. Snatch the first ball in your weaker hand. Catch the second ball in your dominant hand.

This may be starting to get embarrassing. Most people have no trouble getting the first toss into the air, but sometimes the second throw gets heaved away in a nervous rush to vacate a position for the first ball. Since the pattern immediately falls apart once that second throw goes uncatchably straight up or out, or if you get the second ball up and both balls collide in mid-air, or if you muff the first catch, the possibilities for error may seem endless at first.

It may help you to focus by looking only as far as a two-ball crossover as your goal. If you have completed all the previous steps in this chapter but are experiencing difficulty with this one, try giving yourself a reasonable deadline of, say thirty minutes, to accomplish your objective.

Create a vision of a two-ball crossover by studying figure two; panels ten through thirteen are what you are trying to do. Forget about one through nine for now. Imagine that you

Figure 2. TWO-BALLS-TWO-HANDS PATTERN. (1) Rest; (2) right throws ball ①; (3) ball ① passes peak, left throws ball ②; (4) left catches ball ①, ball ② peaking; (5) ball ② passes peak, left throws ball ①; (6) right catches ball ②, ball ① peaking; (7) ball ① passes peak, right throws ball ②; (8) right catches ball ①, ball ② peaking; (9) ball ② passes peak, right throws ball ①; (10) left catches ball ②, ball ① peaking; (11) ball ① passes peak, left throws ball ②; (12) left catches ball ①, ball ② peaking;

have started with ball number one in your right hand, in rest position, and follow through on the rest of the cycle. Concentrate on your vision to make it happen in your hands. The ability to visualize and form something, even if it takes two, or ten, or more half-hour sessions may be the attainable human magic that juggling is not.

Let us review the two-ball crossover

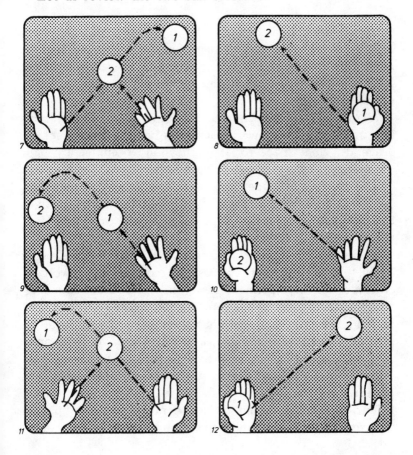

(13) right catches ball ②.

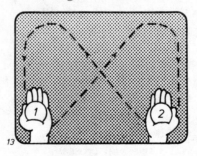

pattern thoroughly. Begin with your rest stance holding a ball in each hand. Practice that much if you feel a need to, and practice calming yourself to reach a place where all things are equal and nothing is pressing on your mind.

When you feel balanced and directed, toss the first ball up in front of your eyes toward your other hand. As that first ball descends, clear space for it in the hand occupied by ball number two by springing the second ball up under the first ball. The stretched open fingers of the hand that held the second ball will then be in excellent position to catch the first ball, and your first hand will have nothing left to do but clasp the second ball, in time.

Those of you who practice directly over a hard surface will know that you are getting closer to controlling a two-ball crossover (or any routine) when your misses start bouncing straighter and landing near enough for you to retrieve them with a quick grab that does not pull you far off your juggling spot. It is even possible to work mistakes into your personal rhythm, playing off the beat of your throws, the drops, the bounces, and your body, until it all becomes one continuous pattern.

Two balls are supposed to trace identically reversed paths. Concentrate on getting them to switch places from your orig-

THE METHOD

inal rest position. Toss one, then the
other as the first begins to come down.
Practice the timing. Make sure that the
balls go up in front of your face. Try to
keep your hands near waist level. Forget
about catches, if you must, but work to
make throws automatic. Then, when
your pitching is down pat, you can concentrate on catching.

When you can accomplish a two-ball
crossover without hitches in your movements, do ten more
two-throw cycles, starting the first with your *weaker* hand,
the next with your stronger hand, the third with the subordinate, and so on. Repeat the cycles ten more times, or
until every one is consistently excellent.

When you feel secure about your two-ball crossover, go
back to look at all of figure two, including panels one through
nine. A two-ball, two-hand routine can go on indefinitely
by simply repeating the patterns as they are shown. But
you can demonstrate your control by stopping cleanly, as the
diagram illustrates. It always feels good to completely direct
your efforts, and it may boost your confidence, which may
help you do anything better. (If you are uninterested in
counting out a preset number of throws to stop at, you may
be swayed by this sidelight: The decorous good sense to end
things more or less gracefully before inevitable misthrows fly
off and skip sloppily out of hand is often regarded by non-
jugglers as skill.)

Practice juggling two balls in two hands until you can keep
doing it for as long as you want to, and stop cleanly before
you miss. Then fling a few alternating one throws, and try
switching back to two-ball juggling. Work on looking only
straight ahead so that you can establish peripheral limits of
your sight, for future reference. And concentrate on making
both of your hands work equally reliably—keep juggling to

render the designations "stronger" or "weaker" terms of convenience instead of certitude.

Take your time with these two-ball patterns. Practice cross-overs and alternating one throws, flipping continuously between the two without stopping or dropping, until you can do it easily. And keep training to make every throw to the same depth, or you will have to learn how to joggle—a hybrid modern sport combining jogging and juggling—as soon as you leave your juggling corner. Standing with your shins against an immovable bed frame is meant to keep you from straining far forward for bad throws and eventually break you of any inclination to throw them. And mid-air collisions may finally teach you to concentrate on consistently pitching up under a ball coming down. Remember: Whenever a ball starts to descend, spring another one up, keeping your throws evenly high and wide on each side, and looking ahead, not at your hands.

You are standing on the threshold of an infinite sport. The exercises in this chapter may seem easy to you. If that is the case, then you are on the right track. If they seem difficult, keep practicing and take heed: Once you become confident with these fundamental skills and competent with these "easy" patterns, as far as juggling is concerned, you have made it.

CHAPTER
12

The Cascade

Three Balls in Two Hands

Please pick up a third ball in whichever hand you want to use for your next throw. (Some people feel they have better control of throws with their "weaker" hand.) Clearly, this complicates matters.

To hold two balls in one hand, slip one ball low down into the heel of your palm. A thumb, pinkie, and ring finger typically curl securely around it. Index and middle fingers stretch back to accommodate another ball, which they hold in place by pressing it up against the first ball. Look at the various illustrations, such as the beginning of the flip sequence and the first panel of the three-ball cascade cycle diagram (figure three), to check the proper positioning for your hands. Some

Figure 3. THREE-BALL CASCADE CYCLE. (1) Rest; (2) right throws ball ①; (3) ball ① passes peak, left throws ball ②; (4) left catches ball ①, ball ② passes peak, right throws ball ③; (5) right catches ball ②, ball ③ passes peak; (6) left catches ball ③.

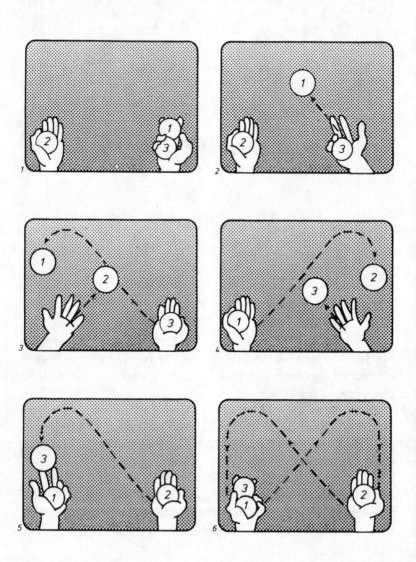

THE METHOD

jugglers prefer a three-finger grip on the top ball, and this is an option for you to consider.

Almost Juggling

Relax in rest position with two balls in your best throwing hand, one ball in your other hand. Once you have established a comfortable grip, even your breathing. Balance your pose. Clear your mind of needless thoughts.

When you feel calm and prepared, spring the odd ball resting on your fingertips up across your face into the top of a bow tie pattern, catching it in the temporary basket sided by the ball in your other hand and its outstretched index and ring fingers. Toss it back, then continue pitching the same ball back and forth in head-high arcs, through its bow tie paces, without disturbing the other balls nestled in the palms of your hands. Take care not to bounce throws off the resting balls; snatch tosses briefly with your fingertips before casting them back up from the inside, catching on the outside, and so on. Working until you can juggle this one-ball cycle may be worthwhile; it is the last piece of information you need to know before creating your own three-ball cascade.

Three-Ball Cascade Juggling

The three-ball cascade is the pattern the little character is juggling in the animated flip sequence in the upper corners of these pages. The basic sequence involves rotating three balls, one at a time, by alternately throwing, throwing-catching, throwing-catching, and so on, with two hands. A ball is always tossed up just as the last one thrown starts to come down.

If you watch the little juggler by flipping through these pages, you may be able to see that he is throwing versions of bow tie outlines with each ball, alternating right- and left-hand tosses and catches within a two-dimensional grid. Without ever moving off his spot, he is controlling a continual exchange of balls, always a ball in one hand and a ball that will arrive at the other hand as one leaves it.

Before making any throws, settle yourself in rest position with the three balls in your hands. Take a long deep breath. Exhale slowly. Take three more deep breaths. Make your wrists limp and shake your hands. Close your eyes for a few seconds. Open and refocus them. Repeat several times.

When you feel well-directed, flick the top ball up off your fingertips across your line of sight toward your subordinate hand. When this first throw begins its descent, pitch the second ball up out of your weaker hand under the incoming first ball in a reciprocal face-high arc, and as soon as it is launched, complete a quick exchange by closing your spread fingers around the rapidly descending first ball. Your second throw should be descending by this time, which means you must clear space for it by springing the *third* ball up under it. Immediately catch the second ball in your empty hand and catch the third ball in the basket of your fingertips and the ball in your other hand. Stop.

You have earned my respect if you succeeded in throwing that last pattern. It is called a three-ball cascade. Congratulate yourself. You were just juggling! All three balls ended up in different spots from where they started—without hitting the floor—and your hands never left your arms!

Seriously, when you stop jumping for joy—or moping, as the case may be—listen to this. Some people, even those who remain perfectly calm practicing every one- and two-ball juggling pattern, have been observed to panic when con-

fronted with what to do with a third ball. The first throw goes up alright, the second too, usually. But despite all the careful training they have had with patient repetitions of every move they will ever need to know to follow this pattern, the sight of that *second* airborne projectile coming toward a hand still holding another ball — while the other hand holds yet *another* ball! — may seem ominous. Some people just fling that third ball straight into a wall, down a street, behind their backs, or out a doorway, anywhere to get rid of it quickly so they can just catch the second throw before it hurts them. Others flail their arms indecisively as balls bounce all around them, or just drop all their balls on the spot, in despair.

Self-protection is a strong urge, but cowardice is never pretty. The road to juggling advancement lies somewhere in between. That it is paved with missed chances is indisputable.

Misses of all sorts are likely to become increasingly common from here on. Big, brawny egos have been known to shrivel into quivering lumps of mushy embarrassment due to public misses. Other droppers turn tail and become early quitters.

Alas, everyone misses — though pros are paid not to at work — and at such moments it seems wiser to laugh than to have a migraine headache, or a stroke, or to break something or someone. Laugh at yourself; go ahead, no one is watching (if you set up your juggling spot as recommended). If you are seeking agreement before letting loose your inhibitions, then yes, I agree with you — a human being can look silly chasing chaotically bouncing balls all over the place. If you were to watch yourself setting up very carefully in rest position, centering yourself, stretching, blinking, taking deep breaths to concentrate on throwing balls up into the air so that you could immediately lose all control of the situation, you might laugh, or cry, but I think it would be better to laugh. And try again. Juggling really can improve your sense of humor, along with your sense of resolve, if you allow it to.

Back to the task at hand, more research may be in order for you to home in on your cascade. Look closely at the flip sequence. Run it through many times, until you can really see juggling happening. Concentrate on watching the hands spring and snatch the balls, and look for the bow tie patterns that the balls trace in the air. Note that the routes the balls follow are not absolutely symmetrical, not perfectly "correct." This is because the little character was drawn from a human model, a juggler with a personal style that veers somewhat from the path of classical perfection. If you are having difficulty mastering a three-ball cascade, you may be trying too hard to be perfect.

As imperfect as our little juggler is, he still manages to demonstrate everything you need to know to learn the cascade. And because the artwork is so skillfully human, the flip sequence illustrates other motions which may look similar to some of the less-than-computer-perfect moves you may be making. If you did not know that such moves are okay, it might cause you worry, which could block the smooth energy flow you need to juggle.

Watch only the right hand in the flip sequence. It springs upward and the fingers stretch open, ejecting the first throw from the lower inside of the bow tie design. Then, in phase, the right hand makes the third throw, catches the second throw, tosses the fifth throw up and exchanges it for the incoming fourth throw, tosses it up in exchange for the incoming sixth throw, and so on. Up and down the hand moves, opening and closing, springing up to release the balls, gripping lightly to catch them. There is relatively little movement in the arm; the hand goes up and down, and moves slightly from side to side, to make throws and catches along the lower edges of the bow tie shape.

Now check the left hand. It covers a broader sort of route, also tossing and snagging along the bow tie outline, but tracing its own small invisible circle in the air to reach throwing and catching points. The left hand has a pronounced swing to its movements, a full looping pattern of its own, while the right hand follows a straighter design.

Think back a few chapters to the mental benefits of juggling. The more strictly efficient right hand is controlled by the left side of the brain—the orderly, mathematical, logical half of the brain. The left hand is directed by the right brain—the creative, imaginative hemisphere. Now consider this: The model for the animated figure was right-handed, and so might have been expected to show a preference for the left side, one might think, by working his dominant right hand most closely to "perfect" juggling form. Just the opposite is the case. With this in mind, your opinion on what the flip scene *says* about handedness, free-will, or the little juggler's competence depends on how you view juggling and yourself.

The little juggler's style says two things to me: Form is less important than just juggling. And be content to *master* gravity; it is futile to try *besting* nature. You are a force of nature.

Establish your easiest going flow within the broad guidelines of "good juggling form," and stick with it until it stops working for you. You will improve with practice. It takes hard work and *years* of daily practice to make a great juggler, but it should not take you that long to learn the three-ball cascade.

For starters, be glad to make a simple three-ball exchange as illustrated in figure three. Count throws if it helps you. Toss one up, two up—catch one, three up—catch two, catch three. And do it again. Reset yourself in the rest position after each three-throw cycle. Reverse direction, starting the cascade with your other hand. Concentrate. Throw balls up under incoming balls. You can do it, although once you can handle a three-ball cascade sequence, you may not be home free yet. Even if you are able to repeat the cycle a few times without dropping, if there are any sudden moves, lunges, or hasty grabs evident in your fundamental routine, you still need more practice before you try out for Clown College.

Keep repeating the basic cascade exchange. It only takes three throws and three catches to get all the balls in different positions from where they started. It is a quick, compact sequence and excellent practice for control. Make sure that you can start solidly with each hand. And if you stop cleanly and return to rest position, even after you are good at throwing the cycle, you will improve quickly. That way, by holding yourself back until you are ready, you can sneak up on the next obvious step of adding more throws, tossing them in only when it feels right, when you *have* to, because if you do not keep going you will burst from anticipation.

The way to add more throws to your cascade at the right time is like this: Spring a first ball up. Spring a second ball up under it from your other hand as the first ball passes its peak, and catch the first ball in that just emptied hand. As the second ball passes its peak, toss a third ball up under it from the hand you started the cascade with, and catch the second ball in the vacant hand. Now, instead of clutching the third throw and stopping, retoss the first ball up (from your other hand this time) after the third ball peaks, then catch the third ball in that empty hand. Toss the second ball up again, snag the first. Throw the third, catch the second, pitch the first, grab the third, and so forth, ad infinitum, if you dare. Once you establish the pattern it can go on until you drop.

In conclusion: Please remember to work on keeping your hands down. The little juggler moves his hands up as high as his armpits—and gets away with it—but he is only a cartoon.

You should know that you should try to keep your hands near waist level. If your throws just seem to naturally carry your hands upward like the little juggler's, meet incoming balls at chest height, okay? But no higher. Wait for the balls to reach you; and they will. Moving up to meet them costs time, and now is when you need all the time you can get to concentrate on aligning the next exchange about to take place.

Focus on the high points and on the consistency of your throws. Keep your bow tie as symmetrical as you can. Here is where practice at lining up catches in advance pays off. You want to be able to shift your attention to the next peak while a catch takes place automatically. Try not to squeeze the balls when you catch them, but shovel them from the lower points of the bow tie to be thrown up along the inside edges of the design.

Vary tosses in two-dimensions only by always throwing up under incoming throws, never throwing forward or straight up into the air. *Throw to the same depth each time.* You want to be able to catch every ball in your hands without straightening your elbows.

Breathe.

Do not grit your teeth, bite your tongue, cross your eyes, tense your neck or jaw or any other part of your body.

Once you learn all the motions, you only need to practice them to smooth them out. In the immediate euphoria of success, you may get carried away and sloppy, but try to work toward good form. If you concentrate on throwing neatly and catching cleanly, you will make rapid progress, and soon you will be juggling without thinking about it at all. Then you will be well on your way to discovering the eternal flow of the basic cascade.

PART
IV

Continuity

NOW THAT YOU KNOW HOW TO DO A THREE-BALL CASCADE, practice until you can do it, and then smooth out your movements. It is possible that controlled consistency with a cascade will eventually become automatic for you. If you concentrate in the beginning, then soon you may be able to perform without thinking about each pattern fragment. When your conscious mind is free of juggling responsibility, you may experience some of the relaxation, meditation, and liberation potentials of commitment to sport.

Or you may want to expand on your rudimentary cascade by tossing higher, wider, or faster throws. You might enjoy testing how quickly your hands can move by lowering your cascade throws so the pattern occurs below shoulder level. Or syncopate your rhythms by tossing an occasional brief, low throw into a high or wide bow tie. An unadorned cascade has an essential purity to it—a simplicity that can be hypnotic—and by slightly varying your rhythms and moves, you might keep busy with it for a long time.

Something different may happen to you; playing with the simple three-ball cascade, achieving reliability and harmony with throws and catches, be they high, wide, or fancy, may put new juggling ideas into your head and open doors for you to previously unimaginable juggling artistry. Some of these thoughts will be covered in the following chapters.

This last section of the book will explain how to do more juggling. Many of the bits have something to do with the cascade or exercises covered prior to it. They all offer additional challenges by presenting fresh ways to use your new skills. If you have patience and desire, these routines can show you that a three-ball cascade is a formative pattern, yet another structural block easily built upon.

The juggling business in the following chapters may come in especially handy if you do any performing. A long flowing cascade volley may be great for you to meditate on but, unless you are a true master, it is probably best not to try to wow an audience with an extended showing of your peaceful centeredness; they might find it a bit dry for entertainment. For shows, many of the following patterns blend nicely with what you already know and may be mixed with it, interweaving different sequences into a broad rhythmic structure to produce diverse and amusing routines.

A three-ball cascade is a symmetrical juggling equation that concentrates focused intent into a soothing work of beautifully consistent change, something that may not be readily found in many areas of living. The following patterns are more of the same. Some may take considerable effort to accomplish; all can give you satisfaction and delight.

There are at least as many ways to combine and intertwine these patterns as there are jugglers.

Express yourself.

JUST JUGGLE!

CHAPTER
13

More Basic Patterns

Let us assume that you can do a three-ball cascade. If you have followed the instructions in this book, you may be well beyond the awkward point where your second or third throw goes skying straight upward or flying straight outward in a rush to make room in your hand for an incoming ball. If you have been practicing, you may be far past mid-air collisions and abrupt gropings in frenzied haste for a ball drifting out of reach. You may know how to chart locations in your mind and aim for juggling within your present range, and your movements, once choppy, may be smoother now that you have learned to establish your own juggling rhythm. If you have learned to respect a display of skill in its purest, most private showings, then you may notice that you are more aware of texture, density, and substance than you were before you knew how to juggle.

If your cascade is still choppier than smooth and flowing, if your throws sometimes fly away from you, or if you feel clumsy throwing a three-ball cascade, you may need more practice before handling these advanced patterns. Ask yourself these questions and answer them honestly before moving along.

Do your throws spring up from the ridge at the base of your fingers?

Do your hands stay down to wait for throws to reach them?

Are you lining up catches at the peaks of balls' flights and letting catches happen automatically while you are concentrating on the next peak and exchange about to take place?

And are you dropping a lot less often than you did at the start?

If you are doing all of these things and are looking for new juggling to do, read on.

Overhand Throws, Half-Reverse Cascade, Reverse Cascade

The next juggling business is a routine you may have imagined you saw if you flipped our little animated juggler through his cascade paces from back to front. Please thumb through the flip sequence backward several times, even if you have done so already.

What you see when you run the flip sequence backwards is a pattern aptly called a reverse cascade. It originates from the same basic rest position as a regular cascade and is characterized by alternating right- and left-hand throws and catches, but it features overhand throws instead of the shoveling underhand throws that you became used to in the regular cascade. These overhand throws are released near the lower outside edge of the typical bow tie cycle and are caught along the lower inside of it, which is exactly the opposite of the regular cascade.

To begin working toward throwing reverse cascades, stand in rest position with just one ball in your favorite hand. Relax yourself and spring the ball up from waist level by turning your wrist out

Figure 4. REVERSE CASCADE CYCLE. (1) Rest; (2) right overthrows ball ①; (3) ball ① passes peak, left overthrows ball ②; (4) left catches ball ①, ball ② passes peak, right overthrow balls ③;

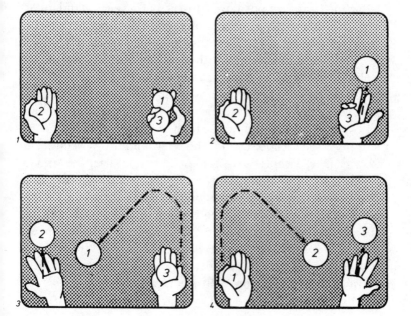

(5) right catches ball ②, ball ③ passes peak; (6) left catches ball ③.

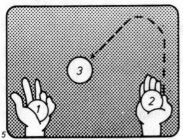

and pitching it overhand. You want the ball to peak in front of your head and land in your other hand, at the opposite lower inside of what will be a bow tie pattern, after you throw the ball back to your first hand the same overhand way.

Work on single tosses until you feel good throwing them, then combine throws to complete an outside-to-inside bow tie cycle. When your overhand cycles with one ball are smooth, pick up another ball.

Starting from rest position with one ball in each hand, overhand the first ball up from your chosen hand. After that throw passes its peak, toss the second ball up *over* it. Catch the first ball immediately with your subordinate hand and catch the second ball with your first hand.

Overhand throws may feel awkward after regular cascade work, so it may be smart to move up from these humble one- and two-ball beginnings rather than to jump right into a complete reverse cascade. Oddly, the overhand throw is closer to the way most people were taught to throw than the under- hand shoveling motion used for the regular cascade. But now it may seem like a new move, and it might throw you off the track before it falls into place for you.

When you feel comfortable making overhand two-ball cross- overs, you may want to start working overhand throws into a regular cascade to add variety to your routines and to give you more practice before you attempt a complete reverse. Start by picking out a red ball, or a striped one, or any clearly

marked ball. Juggle a regular cascade, but every time the marked ball is thrown from your dominant hand, make it an overhand toss. Work on this single change until you feel confident flicking the marked ball up over an incoming ball each time it comes around to your dominant side.

Next, move from pitching your marked ball overhand from your dominant hand only to throwing it overhand every time you fling it up from either hand. And once you can manage that, work on making every right-hand toss an overthrow. This is a nifty-looking pattern called a half-reverse cascade. And when you have it down on your right side, switch over to your left and make every left-handed send-off an overhand toss, while your right hand continues to spring up regular cascade underhand throws.

Your ultimate objective with practicing overhand throws is to be able to juggle an entire pattern of them. A full reverse cascade cycle is illustrated in figure four. In this sequence, all throws are overhanded from the lower outside of the bow tie cycle and caught at the lower inside of the design.

Keep practicing overhand throws, half-reverse cascades, and reverse cascades until the patterns are easy for you to follow and you can switch fluidly back and forth between them and regular cascades. Then you will be ready to move on to overhand catches, also known as clawing. Clawing looks great, works neatly into a regular cascade, and gives you another variable to work with in mixing moves and patterns to create your own juggling routines.

Clawing

To begin, pick a marked ball, again, and your best *catching* hand to first claw with. From a relaxed rest position, spring up a regular one-ball bow tie pattern from your *other* hand, but before the marked ball can be caught in a regular manner (by waiting for it to land in your hand), reach up to eye level with your chosen "claw," flipping your hand over as you raise it, and make an overhand grab of the ball by clamping down *over* it as it passes the peak of its flight. Figure five illustrates this move. To complete a lopsided bow tie cycle, promptly flick the ball back up with a lift up and a slight inward turn of your wrist.

Work with one ball and one hand until you can feel what clawing is like. You need to bring your hand up to meet the ball, so you will have to reset your body and mind to accommodate that change from everything you have learned up to now. Practice clawing catches every time the ball approaches your best catching hand. Grab throws at eye level, but do not let your hand begin its normal, gravity-aided descent toward

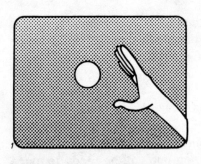

Figure 5. CLAWING. (1) Hand reaches up; (2) closes over ball; (3) wrist turns in to throw ball back up.

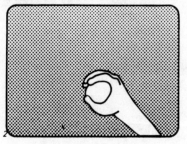

rest position. Instead, lift your wrist back up and turn it inward slightly to spring the ball back up toward your other hand. After you are clawing easily with one hand, switch to your other hand. When you can claw with either hand, you will be ready to add clawing grabs to your cascade routines.

Start by clawing only the one marked ball with one hand. Throw a regular cascade, but each time the marked ball approaches your claw, reach up, grab it out of the air, and flick it back up into the flow of the routine. Switch, and make clawing grabs with your other hand only. Then, claw the marked ball with both hands, every time it comes around, eventually working up to clawing every throw, which, as you will see, is an excellent way to demonstrate how frantic a three-ball cascade can become. Clawing is fun to do, and it looks amazing to anyone watching you juggle. Once you master it, you can start combining it with regular, half-reverse, and reverse cascades into virtually infinite varieties of three-ball routines.

The Shower

To do this next routine, you need to make some excellent overhand throws with at least one of your hands. In a shower cycle, one hand does all the throwing and each throw is an overthrow. Your other hand will only catch and pass balls across your body to the throwing hand.

The shower is the pattern that most people who make believe they know how to juggle do badly. It is completely different from the cascade, not a variation of it. Only one hand throws balls up, the other catches and passes balls laterally, and the balls move in a circular outline instead of a bow tie design. Since each hand must practice separate skills for showering, the notions about balance that you have worked to develop may be challenged by it. A three-ball shower is not as easy to do as it looks; it is more difficult for most people than a regular cascade and may take you longer to learn. But while you work through it, think of this: School-girls on Tonga in the South Pacific routinely shower five things. If you are adept at the juggling routines covered so far, a three-ball shower is attainable.

Basic preparation for showering is to put two balls in your best throwing hand in rest position. When you are calm and focused, overhand the top ball up in front of your head to-ward your other hand, but this time, as the ball *approaches* the top of its arc, on the *upswing* of its flight, overthrow the second ball up after it along an identical path. The trick here is to throw balls as quickly and consistently as you can. Catch the first throw, then the second in your other hand.

When your throws and catches are accurate, start laterally passing, not throwing, but handing back each ball as soon as it is caught by pushing it across your stomach toward your throwing hand. Rethrow each passed ball as soon as your throwing hand grabs it. This is how people who do not know how to do it "juggle," but for you, this is just a warm-up exercise.

The moves for a shower are similar to a half-reverse cas-cade, but in a shower you pass balls straight across your body instead of underhanding them up and across to be over-handed back. The difference becomes apparent when you try to shower three balls. The half-reverse cascade has a relatively leisurely tempo compared to a three-ball shower which must be thrown faster and, therefore, more precisely than any of the patterns you have worked on already.

To throw a three-ball shower, first look at figure six, to see what the moves look like. Then assume the rest position with two balls in your best throwing hand, one in the other.

Compose yourself and overhand the top ball up. Quickly overhand the second ball after it, and pass the third ball across to your throwing hand. Hold it there and immediately return your catching hand to its rest position to catch the first throw, and then the second. Stop. Work on that for awhile.

A three-ball shower is swift business to care for. Every catch must be passed as soon as it lands and rethrown as it touches your throwing hand. The only variable that gives you any flexibility is the length of the arcs that you throw. If you can control long tosses, hold your hands extra far apart and throw balls up over your head to give yourself more time to catch and pass.

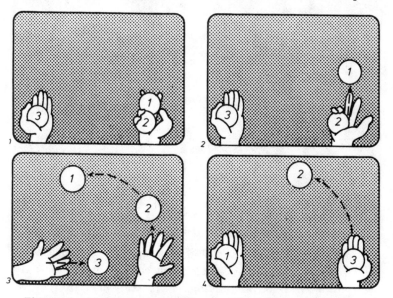

Figure 6. SHOWER PATTERN. (1) Rest; (2) right overthrows ball ①; (3) right overthrows ball ②, ball ① peaking, left passes ball ③; (4) right receives ball ③, ball ② rising, left catches ball ①;

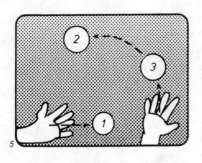

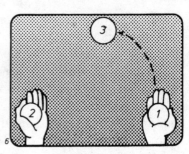

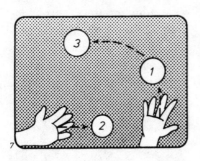

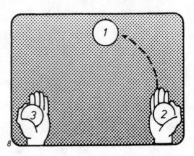

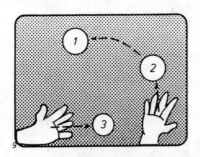

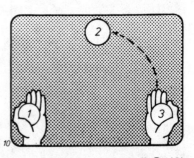

(5) right overthrows ball ③, ball ② peaking, left passes ball ①; (6) right receives ball ①, ball ③ rising, left catches ball ②; (7) right overthrows ball ①, ball ③ peaking, left passes ball ②; (8) right receives ball ②, ball ① rising, left catches ball ③; (9) right overthrows ball ②, ball ① peaking, left passes ball ③; (10) right receives ball ③, ball ② rising, left catches ball ①;

To keep a shower pattern flowing, just keep throwing as fast as you can and passing as soon as you make catches. Study figure six, and watch other jugglers for pointers. Having two balls in the air at all times is what makes a shower tricky to do, though it is possible. Remember those Tongan schoolgirls, and keep practicing.

Floor Bounces

Floor bounces are your reward for working on the difficult three-ball shower; they are comparatively easy and fun to do. For this bit, only good bouncing balls will do. Do not attempt floor bounces with beanbags, fruit, rolled-up socks, eggs, kittens, knives, and so on.

It is time for you to step away from your juggling bed, if you have not done so already. Find a small square of hard flooring to practice on. Tile floors, solid hardwood or linoleum floors, cement or asphalt surfaces will generally work if they are level and fairly smooth. Undulating, gouged or rough surfaces will adversely affect floor bounces.

You need only a three-by-three-foot square to stand in to

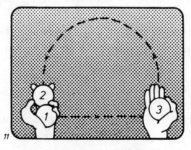

(11) left catches ball ②.

MORE BASIC PATTERNS

127

throw floor bounces, but it is wise to clear the surrounding area as well. Your first bounces with fast, resilient juggling balls may fly up with greater velocity than you might anticipate. They can break things or bop you by bounding up into your face, if you are not careful.

Once you have set up a safe spot for floor bounces, settle yourself with one ball in your dominant hand in rest position. Clasp the ball snugly and turn your hand over, so your palm faces down. Using the same springing motion as for underhand throws, without cocking your wrist, direct the ball down to a point you are focusing on midway between your feet, so that it bounces up to your other palm-down hand. The angle that you throw the ball down will be exactly the same way it returns to your other hand, so if your stance is balanced and your bounce on line, the ball will almost magically come back to your waiting hand without your having to move. Bounce it back to your dominant hand.

To add a second ball, throw it down from your weaker hand to the *outside* of the bounce coming up from your dominant hand, as soon as that first bounce starts up from the floor. Catch the first bounce in your weaker hand, the second bounce in your dominant one. This two-ball exchange can give you a good feel for floor bounces.

Add a third ball by holding two balls in your dominant hand, one in your other hand. Proceed to do a two-ball floor bounce by flicking your first throw off your fingertips, but when the second bounce starts up from the floor, throw the third ball down to the outside of it from your dominant hand. Catch the upcoming second bounce with your dominant hand. Catch the third bounce with your weaker hand (which should be holding the first ball).

Figure seven illustrates a floor bounce cycle. Remember to bounce balls to the outside of balls coming up from the floor, and simply continue throwing bounces down—rethrow the first ball as the third comes up, the second as the first does, and so on — if you want to keep the routine going longer than for three throws.

"Holding-Hands" Juggling

To conclude this chapter, the following is one of the simplest patterns you can do to set yourself off on many hours of juggling challenges and benefits. This bit calls for a partner and is a good

Figure 7. FLOOR BOUNCE CYCLE. (1) Rest with hands facing *down*; (2) right throws ball ① down; (3) ball ① hits floor and starts *up*, left throws ball ② down; (4) left catches ball ①, ball ② hits floor and starts up, right throws ball ③ down;

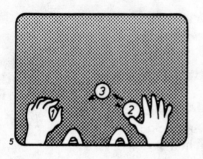

(5) right catches ball ②, ball ③ hits floor and starts up; (6) left catches ball ③.

ploy to get a friend interested in juggling so you can have someone to work additional partner's routines with. Until now, a partner has been a luxury, but for this bit, another juggler is essential. The trick is this: Stand side by side with your partner so that each of you can act as one arm of a wide-bodied juggler tossing a three-ball cascade. Some partners hold hands. Others put their arms around each other's back or twist their arms behind their own backs, but the two of you will need to stand shoulder to shoulder to juggle with your outer arms only. Being physically close is just part of this bit; you and your partner will have to tap into each other's private rhythms to become juggling partners.

To accomplish this hard-looking routine, start with two balls in your free hand, one ball in your partner's. Toss your normal underhand throw up into the first phase of a regular bow tie cycle, but make sure you throw it hard enough to reach your partner's free hand. When that first ball passes its peak between your two heads, your partner underhands ball number two into the start of its normal cycle and catches ball number one, thrown by you. You, on the other hand, are holding the third ball, which you release before you catch ball two, and your partner springs ball one back up before catching ball three, and so forth.

If you and your partner get to be skilled at juggling cascades

while holding hands, you might want to try mixing in overhand throws with the regular pattern. See if you can juggle up a half-reverse cascade, then a full reverse. Perhaps you can juggle a "holding-hands" shower, or work up planned multi-pattern routines. Maybe the two of you can progress to a point where you can spontaneously improvise varying patterns in mid-juggle, just the way a single well-balanced brain might operate! Working with a partner increases your chances to figure out more than you might alone. Cooperation is the key; juggling is the hand that opens the door.

CHAPTER
14

Upping the Limits

If you have juggled this far and mastered the exercises this book has covered, you may be hooked on a new pastime. If a basic cascade, reverse cascades, clawing, floor bounces, and even an astonishingly rapid shower progression are second nature to you, and your appetite for juggling is barely whetted, try some of the following juggling patterns.

Two Balls in One Hand

Juggling two balls in one hand is where you will finally be unable to compensate for weaknesses in your subordinate hand. Three-ball cascades, bounces, and all the other patterns you have worked on involve both hands in alternating rhythms, but for this routine, you will only use one hand at a time. Your subordinate hand will no longer be able to reflexively mimic your stronger hand, and will thus have a chance to show how well developed it has become on its own.

Learning to juggle two balls in one hand can require a lot of legwork, so begin by putting two balls in your stronger hand and settling yourself in your corner spot over your juggling bed. Collect your energies and consider your objective. You are going to want to spring two balls up in sequence, and catch both, using only one hand.

Your throws will have to be consistent and exacting. If you divide the number of balls by the number of hands used to juggle them, you will find that juggling two balls in one hand is more work for one hand to do than juggling three balls is for two hands. This means that juggling two balls in one hand involves faster exchanges than a three-ball cascade, and your margin for error will be narrowed correspondingly. Reaching or chasing off-line throws may make it difficult or impossible to catch the next ball in place, so tosses need to be as nearly identical as you can make them.

To juggle two balls in one hand, throw one ball up into the air, and when it reaches its highest point of flight at face level, let the second ball fly up after it. The first throw is then caught in the same hand that threw it and rethrown as the second ball peaks, and so on.

There are at least three distinct routes that two balls being

Figure 8. TWO-BALLS-ONE-HAND-/CLOCKWISE CYCLE. (1) Rest; (2) right throws ball ①; (3) ball ① passes peak, right throws ball ②; (4) right catches ball ①, ball ② peaking; (5) right catches ball ②.

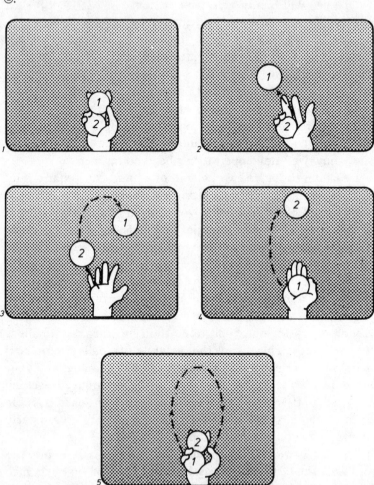

juggled by one hand may adhere to. The first is a clockwise cyclical pattern in which two balls cover identical oval paths in a clockwise direction (see figure eight).

The second possibility is a counter-clockwise cycle in which the balls go exactly the opposite oval way (figure nine).

And the third option is a parallel elevator pattern in which two balls are sprung straight up into the air side by side. A juggler's hand shifts slightly from place to place to spring and catch the balls in this sequence (figure ten).

Figure 9. TWO-BALLS-ONE-HAND/COUNTERCLOCKWISE CYCLE. (1) Rest; (2) left throws ball ①; (3) ball ① passes peak, left throws ball ②; (4) left catches ball ①, ball ② peaking;

(5) left catches ball ②.

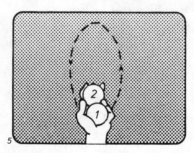

Figure 10. TWO-BALLS-ONE-HAND/ELEVATOR PATTERN. (1) Rest; (2) right throws ball ①; (3) ball ① passes peak, right throws ball ②; (4) right catches ball ①, ball ② peaking; (5) ball ② passes peak, right throws ball ①; (6) right catches ball ②, ball ① peaking; (7) ball ① passes peak, right throws ball ②; (8) right catches ball ①, ball ② peaking;

Before beginning any of the cycles, it may be helpful for you to think about a characteristic of juggling two balls in one hand: Cycling balls up in the same direction from each hand calls for different types of throws. A clockwise right-hand cycle uses underhand throws. A clockwise left-hand cycle uses overhand throws. This may take some getting used to.

To start the cycles, ease yourself into rest position with one ball in your right hand. Practice springing the lone ball up into the air in a narrow clockwise oval that ends back in your right hand, which should be still in rest position. The underhand toss

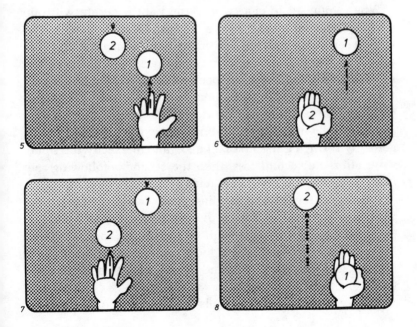

(9) right catches ball ②.

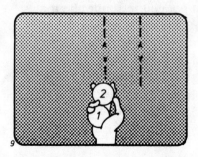

takes more wrist action than the other throws you have worked on, though your objective, with practice, is to move your hand as little as possible. After you get the feel of a clockwise circular throw, add a second ball to the same hand and throw the same single-ball cycle off your fingertips with the new ball remaining pressed against the heel of your palm.

When your single clockwise throws are accurate with an extra ball in your hand, you are ready to juggle both balls. Do this by centering yourself in rest position, tossing the first ball up off your fingertips, and springing the second ball up after it, as that first ball passes its peak at the top of the thin oval. Catch the first ball in your palm. Catch the second in your fingers. That is all there is to it. Practice the two throws for awhile. And when you feel prepared, try to keep the pattern going by springing the first ball up again, in exactly the same way, after the second toss, then the second refollowing the first up again, and just keep going.

When you feel strong juggling a two-ball clockwise cycle with your right hand, switch over to your left hand and repeat the practice process with one change: Toss left-hand throws in a counterclockwise loop, underhanding tosses just as you did with your right hand, working up to a continuous two-ball cycle.

After you can juggle two balls in either hand using underhand throws, train each hand to juggle two balls using overhand throws. Follow the same practice scheme. Work with your right hand first, tossing counter-clockwise cycles, then with your left hand flinging clockwise ovals. Continue to spring a ball up as the last throw passes its peak, and try to keep balls following along the same route through the air, as if they were locked on an invisible track.

Practice both cycles with each hand, and when you feel satisfied with your control, try a parallel elevator pattern like this: Place two balls in your right hand. Flip the first ball straight up off your fingers to head height. As the toss rises, shift your hand a few inches toward your middle. When the throw passes its peak, spring the second ball straight up, off the base of your fingers, to the left of the ball on the way down. After releasing the second ball, shift back smoothly to the right, catch the first ball, and slip back over to the left, to snag the second throw.

Practice two parallel throws for awhile, then work on keeping the pattern going longer by always springing a ball back up almost as soon as you catch it, just as the ball in the air is passing its peak. One ball is always supposed to be rising as the other is coming down next to it, just like parallel ascending and descending elevators, which means that you can only hold on to each ball for about as long as it takes a throw to cover one-half the length of one side of the elevator shaft. Excellent throws will travel no more than three or four inches apart, and your hand is supposed to rapidly cover that distance between each throw and catch.

Switch to your left hand after your right one is good at juggling a parallel cycle, and practice until both hands are equally skilled at it. At that point, you may want to try moving from one two-ball pattern to another without stopping. Start juggling clockwise cycles, and switch off to a parallel elevator pattern, and over to a counterclockwise cycle, or any combinations you can dream up.

It will be important for you to become equally adept at all these two-balls-in-one-hand patterns with either hand if you wish to eventually step up to juggling four balls, which is actually juggling two balls in each hand at the same time. For four-ball juggling, both hands must be equally strong and your mind and eyes need to keep track of two essentially separate routines at the same time; exchanges happen faster and more independently than in a three-ball cascade, which encompasses both hands alternatively in one interwoven pattern. Keep practicing two balls in one hand until each of your hands feels sure and competent, with at least one of the cycle patterns, before moving on.

The last step up, to help ease you into juggling four balls, is juggling two and one, which is three-ball juggling with two balls in one hand and one in the other. It calls for timing very close to the same as four-ball juggling. Juggling two and one can be done in numerous ways based on juggling any of the two-balls-in-one-hand patterns in either hand at various tempos. The following instructions detail two different cycles and rhythmic possibilities.

A staggered two-and-one cycle is the one I consider easiest since it feels most like a regular cascade. Start in rest position with two balls in your dominant hand, one in your other. You will be throwing alternatively with each hand, just as in a regular cascade, but the balls will not cross paths. Look at figure eleven. You may be able to see that this calls for uncascade-like timing. The idea is to throw an inside-to-outside two-balls-in-one-hand cycle—clockwise with a dominant right hand (as illustrated in figure eleven), counter with a dominant left—and in-between-circling throws, juggle a single ball in your other hand.

The way it goes for right-handers is like this: Right throw, left throw, right throw-catch, left catch, right throw-catch, left throw, and so forth. The left-hand throw may simply be tossed straight up and down, there is no need to loop it out. Practice to throw the single ball to the same height as your clockwise throws to keep your balance and timing together. For left-handers, please substitute left for right, and vice-versa in the equation.

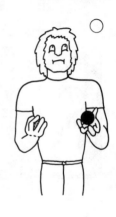

After you work on a two-and-one staggered cycle, starting with either hand holding two balls, the second two-and-one sequence, illustrated in figure twelve, is a half-simultaneous parallel pattern.

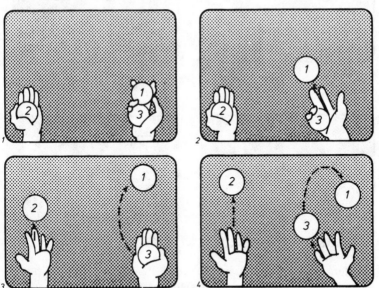

Figure 11. TWO-AND-ONE/STAGGERED PATTERN. (1) Rest; (2) right throws ball ①; (3) ball ① peaking, left throws ball ②; (4) ball ① passes peak, right throws ball ③, ball ② peaking;

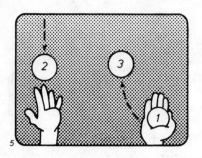
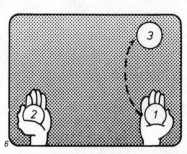

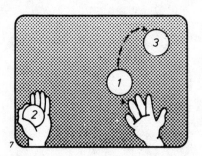
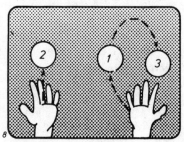

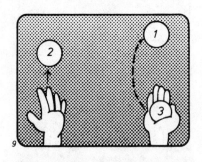
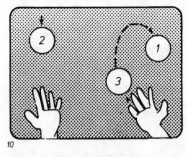

(5) right catches ball ①, ball ③ rising, ball ② descending; (6) left catches ball ②, ball ③ peaking; (7) ball ③ passes peak, right throws ball ①; (8) left throws ball ②, ball ③ descending, ball ① rising; (9) right catches ball ③, ball ① peaking, ball ② rising; (10) ball ① passes peak, right throws ball ③, ball ② descending.

CONTINUITY

Holding two balls in your dominant hand, one in your other, in rest position, you will want to toss up a two-ball parallel elevator pattern in one hand and spring the single ball straight up from your other hand, at the same time as, and also parallel to, the first two-ball throw. It goes like this: Right and left throw (same time), right throw, right and left catch, right and left throw, right catch, right throw, and so on.

I think it is easiest to toss the first throw from the dominant hand up the outer elevator shaft, and the single throw, from the other hand, up the inner column. But feel free to experiment, to reverse hands, and to figure out more ways you can do two-and-one combinations, at any tempo, with either

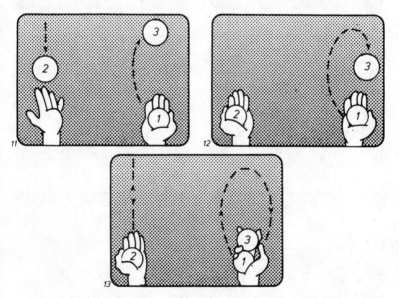

(11) right catches ball ①, ball ③ peaking, ball ② descending; (12) right catches ball ①, ball ③ peaking; (13) right catches ball ③.

Figure 12. TWO-AND-ONE/ELEVATOR PATTERN. (1) Rest; (2) left throws ball ②, right throws ball ①; (3) ball ② passes peak, ball ① passes peak, right throws ball ③; (4) left catches ball ②, right catches ball ①, ball ③ peaking; (5) ball ③ passes peak, left throws ball ②, right throws ball ①; (6) right catches ball ③, ball ② peaking, ball ① peaking; (7) ball ② passes peak, ball ① passes peak, right throws ball ③; (8) left catches ball ②, right catches ①, ball ③ peaking; (9) ball ③ passes peak; (10) right catches ball ③.

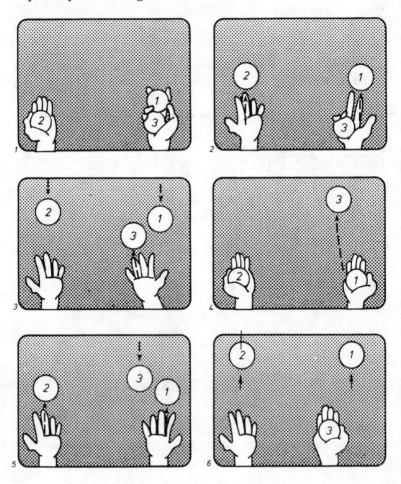

hand holding two balls. If you get sharp on two-and-one cycles, four-ball juggling may be easy for you to pick up.

Four-Ball Juggling

You may combine any two of the two-balls-in-one-hand patterns that you like to accomplish four-ball juggling. The way you put the patterns together is up to you, though there are certain combos that may seem simpler to work with than others. Again, whatever patterns you choose have to be thrown accurately, with special care to keep balls moving regularly within your reach from a rest position. Deviations in the paths the balls follow will get you

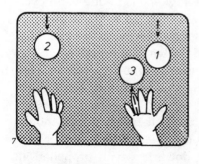

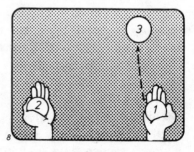

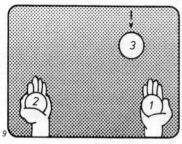

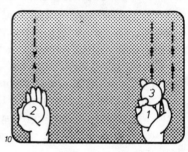

moving after them, so that even if one hand is juggling two balls neatly, bad throws from the other hand might pull you far enough away from rest position to ruin the four-ball pattern. Both two-ball patterns must be consistent to accomplish a four-ball juggle of any continuous duration, and this is what makes the patterns difficult.

We will start with a staggered rhythm. It will give you a fraction of a second between moves on either side of your body and may be the most accessible way to begin juggling four balls.

To throw a four-ball staggered cycle, hold two balls in each hand in rest position. Clear your head thoroughly of distractions for your juggling will need all your attention.

You will be working on alternating a counterclockwise, two-balls-in-one-hand cycle in your left hand, with a clockwise, two-in-one-right-hand cycle. The idea is to combine balanced, underhand throws from each side.

The way to do this is to start a two-balls-in-one-hand cycle with your dominant hand, and when your first throw *approaches* its peak, begin the opposite cycle with your other hand. If you start with your right hand, the pattern will go like this: Right throw, left throw, right throw-catch, left throw-catch, right throw-catch, and so on (see figure thirteen).

This really is the *easiest* of the four-ball patterns, though you may not think so after you have spent the better part of your practice time tracking down lost balls propelled all over the place by mid-air collisions. One tip here is to stand over a bed, and another is throw accurately.

It is impossible to accomplish any four-ball pattern without excellent, controlled throws, and to guarantee consistency, you may have to go back to practicing two balls in each hand at a time. Once each hand's throws are predictably on line, you simply have to evenly resplit the brain halves you finally got working so well together after all your previous juggling practice.

The way to do this is to study figure thirteen, keep throwing and thinking, and figure out some of the other four-ball possibilities for a broader perspective on the task. For instance, keep juggling the same counterclockwise left- and clockwise-right way, so both hands can continue throwing underthrows, but try throwing and catching simultaneously with both hands, as illustrated in figure fourteen.

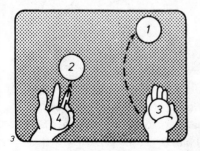
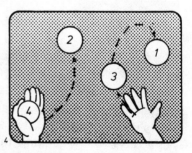

Figure 13. FOUR-BALL/STAGGERED PATTERN. (1) Rest; (2) right throws ball ①; (3) ball ① peaking, left throws ball ②; (4) ball ① passes peak, right throws ball ③, ball ② rising;

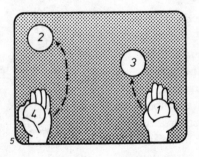
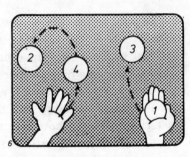

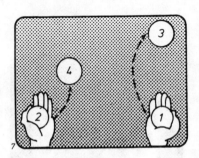
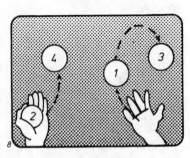

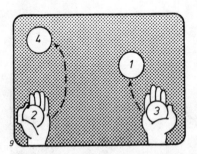
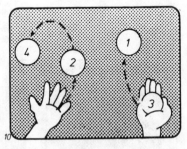

(5) right catches ball ①, ball ③ rising, ball ② peaking; (6) ball ②
passes peak, left throws ball ④, ball ③ rising; (7) left catches ball ②,
ball ④ rising, ball ③ peaking; (8) ball ③ passes peak, right throws
ball ①, ball ④ rising; (9) right catches ball ③, ball ① rising, ball ④
peaking; (10) ball ④ passes peak, left throws ball ②, ball ① rising;

CONTINUITY

This pattern may not look like much of a challenge, but it might be more difficult than an alternating four-ball sequence, since it requires that both hands be separately faultless at exactly the same moment. The balls you throw are supposed to look as if they are connected to each other as they rise and fall evenly into your carefully synchronized hands. If, for example, concurrent throws fly up to different heights, you will have to be able to switch in midsequence from a staggering to a staggered rhythm — or you will lose control of the pattern, when your next throws are out of time, or when you flub the following catches too, if you can stay with the runaway cycle for that long.

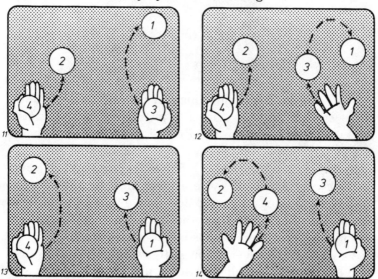

(11) left catches ball ④, ball ① peaking, ball ② rising; **(12)** ball ① passes peak, right throws ball ③, ball ② rising; **(13)** right catches ball ①, ball ② peaking, ball ③ rising; **(14)** ball ② passes peak, left throws ball ④, ball ③ rising;

(15) left catches ball ②, ball ③ peaking, ball ④ rising; (16) ball ③ passes peak, ball ④ peaking; (17) right catches ball ③, left catches ball ④.

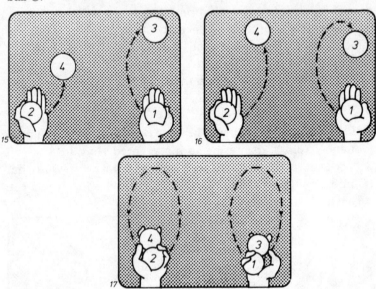

Other possibilities for juggling four balls would be throwing either simultaneous or staggered parallel elevator patterns, clockwise cycles, or counterclockwise cycles, with both hands at the same time, or by reversing your original two-hand split, juggling a clockwise left-hand cycle with a counterclockwise right-hand cycle, so that all your pitches cycle toward the inside. Or you could throw a four-ball crossover pattern, which differs from the others in that it does not encompass separate two-balls-in-one-hand patterns.

A four-ball crossover involves throwing one ball up from each hand, either simultaneously or in staggered tempo, and crossing them in mid-air on the way to each opposite hand, so you can exchange them with the two still in your hands.

First, practice throwing two balls up at a time—one under the other—into simultaneous underhand bow tie cycles.

CONTINUITY

Throw and catch at the same time with each hand. This may feel strange. Underhand the next two balls up at the same time, as the first throws peak. Catch the first throws, and continue crossing bow ties at the same time. Try to keep your hands from spreading impossibly wide in opposite directions to catch bad throws, and to throw balls without mid-air collisions as they cross.

Figure 14. FOUR-BALL/OPPOSING CYCLES. (1) Rest; (2) left throws ball ②, right throws ball ①; (3) ball ② passes peak, ball ③ passes peak, left throws ball ④, right throws ball ①; (4) left catches ball ②, right catches ball ①, ball ④ peaking, ball ③ peaking;

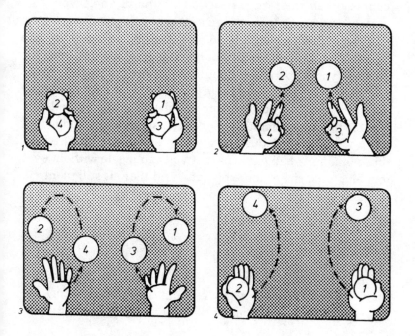

(5) left catches ball ④, right catches ball ③.

As for a four-ball staggered crossover, the pattern approaches the inspirational, encompassing most of the information in this book. If you can do everything else up to this point, then you can probably figure it out for yourself. If you cannot do all the rest, instruction will hardly help you.

Four-ball juggling is as high as this book goes into numbers juggling. The more objects you juggle, the less flexibility you have for experimentation; when you juggle five, six, or seven objects, you experience diminishing time and space to do anything but send props up into the air, exactly where they *must* travel. Juggling greater numbers of things calls for greater precision than three- or four-ball juggling, and leaves less room for individual creativity. There are hundreds of three- and four-ball patterns that you can juggle without ever touching five, six, or more objects. And there is still plenty of fun you can have with a basic cascade.

Clubs

Clubs look difficult to juggle—and seem as if they could really clobber you—but modern plastic clubs (or pins) are lightweight and may actually be a relief to juggle after working with four balls. Step outside to juggle clubs; they are considerably larger than balls and, at first, you will need more head-room to work with them (though you will be doing well when you can juggle clubs under an eight-foot ceiling).

In rest position, grip the neck of a club across the base of your fingers with your thumb pointing toward the fat part of it. You want to *swing* the club around from the lower outside of a bow tie cycle, in order to release it on the way up the lower inside edge of the design.

Practice one throw by swinging the club around and flinging it straight up, so that its base rises first and the whole club flips over once in the air before returning to the same hand. Clubs can really fly away from you, so go easy at first. If you throw the club too high and it flips more than once, your chances of catching it by the neck and continuing to juggle smoothly are slight.

Once you get used to the feel of a club in your dominant hand, switch hands. When both hands can throw club flips easily, complete a one-club bow tie cycle between them, concentrating on turning the club over only once in the air during each throw. The club may go up over your head for now, as long as it lands at the lower outside point of the bow tie, where you can catch it and swing it around the lower inside line, to flip it back up again.

After one throw, work on a two-club crossover. With a club in each hand, alternate throws in bow tie designs by flipping one club up, and as it turns in the air and begins its descent, tossing the other club up under it in its own bow tie. When you can cross two clubs, grab a third one. Hold two in your dominant hand by gripping one neck between your thumb and forefinger, and the other against your three open fingers, held in place by the overlapping tip of your thumb.

To start a three-club cascade, flip the first toss up off your fingertips, exactly the same as for a three-ball cascade.

One thing to guard against is a natural inclination that many people seem to have for throwing clubs far out in front of themselves for self-protection. Rely on your three-ball juggling experience to tell you when your moves are consistent enough for your safety; the best way for you to handle the clubs will be readily apparent to you, if not quite so rapidly mastered.

Rings

After ball juggling and your entree into club work, rings (or hoops) should be easy for you to juggle. Some pros rate these as the easiest of the basic juggling objects to use, and you may throw many two-, three-, or four-ball patterns with rings (forget floor bounces); the main difference is that you will need to swing your arm up to *spin* rings up in front of your face. It is usually easy for a ball juggler to throw a three-ring cascade, or to juggle two rings in one hand. Try it. It really is pretty easy.

Ball Passing

The last instructions in this book call for juggling with a partner, which is similar, in some ways, to playing music with someone. Both acts require basic skills to maintain the integrity of your efforts and extra sensitivity; if you and your partner can tune synchronistically into each other's movements, your independent actions may balance together into a greater harmony.

You can start to practice ball passing without a partner. All you have to do is bounce balls off a side of a building, racquetball court, or any solid, preferably exterior, wall.

Wall bounces differ from real partners juggling in that they cross diagonally in front of your body to reach your other hand, while real partners work proceeds from your right hand to your partner's left, and vice versa, calling for straight throws across.

But a wall can be a partner if you do not have a live one, so assume your rest position about three to four feet away from your chosen barrier. Throw up a regular cascade, but on your third throw, toss the ball diagonally outward against the wall. As it hits the wall, approximating the normal peak of a regularly thrown ball, underhand your next toss up, as you normally would, and reach up to claw the incoming wall bounce. Grab the bounced ball and continue the cascade pattern with a normal exchange of balls in your other hand. Bounce as often as you like until you get into a rhythm you are comfortable with, and work to keep the regular cascade going without interruption.

To start passing balls to a partner, calm down. Both of you should warm up your individual cascades, then stand facing each other about five feet apart. Make sure you both start with two balls in the *same* hand. Work on throwing simultaneous cascades. Your timing must be synchronized or your passes will fall. To help your timing gel, count down together to start, and count throws out loud.

When you are easily juggling together, stop. Then start your cascades in your right hands at the same time, and on the count of five, each pass your right-hand throw across to your partner's left hand. Treat the pass as a normal throw and toss up your next (left-hand) throw *before* you claw the incoming pass. Keep juggling if you can, after clawing the pass, by making a regular right-hand throw and catch exchange, and if you are both juggling on the next five-count, pass again, and again the next time the count comes around.

The extra movements and careful rhythmic symmetry needed to pass balls, multiplied by two jugglers trying to learn them, can equal a sizable chunk of time to master ball passing. It can be time well spent. Once you are able to pass balls, there are hoops and clubs to pass too, and infinite passing patterns that you and your partner, or more partners, can work on. For now, try passing every other right-hand throw, then make every right hand throw a pass, if you can. Make your own passing patterns as fast or as slow as you and your partner like, as complex or simple as you care for.

Always remember that passes are supposed to keep time with your regular cascade throws and peak in the air between partners at the same head level as regular throws. Keep your elbows in as much as possible to prevent throws from going wild, rather than straight out in front of you. Partners juggling takes more than patience; it calls for completely fluid sympathy between you and your partner. Telepathy might help too. Work at it. If you pace yourselves together, count throws and concentrate, the two of you may soon be juggling up storms of balls, hoops, clubs, or flowerpots, if you wish, and having twice as much fun in the bargain.

CHAPTER
15

Vistas

There are many other juggling patterns to be learned. You might discover some on your own while performing exercises outlined in this book. Others may seem to occur to you spontaneously at a later date, or perhaps another juggler will show you things that you had not thought of before. For now, though, what is mainly important is that if you have mastered a three-ball cascade, you deserve praise. You have learned something new! Bravo!

If, however, congratulations are not yet in order, you may

need more time with basics. There is no substitute for practice. Leaf through the flip sequence and dissect a three-ball cascade frame by frame if you need to. Look at the cycle diagrams and re-read instructional material step by step. You are in control. Juggling balls travel because you propel them.

What, Me Juggle?

Poised, self-confident juggling progress evolves from within. Contented students find encouragement in their hearts and minds, not from other people or things, and this self-control can also help a juggler concentrate on learning to become attentive and relaxed at the same time. By clearing away distractions and irrelevancies, some jugglers may uncover a place where all extremes can come full circle, where wisdom and foolishness, boredom and bliss become one and each other, losing distinction and authority all at once.

Repetitive practice of a three-ball cascade has been known to induce peaceful states approximating personal stability. You might connect that inner calm with your experience of how good juggling makes you feel as it helps you balance your energies. Quirks, mannerisms, and conflicting habits that jugglers need to put aside to learn new patterns may help quiet the voices of their demons. The ability to defocus on yourself and stay balanced might be as important to challenging passing routines, such as growing up, as it is to juggling.

At the same time, you alone marshal the strengths needed to juggle, and this gives you a chance to consistently create something harmonious that can be touched and seen, that infringes on no one's space or time and takes nothing away from anyone. By accomplishing your objective, you show how easily you can be alone, handle yourself, and pick up a new trick or two along a productive, satisfying, solitary way.

How Much More Mixed-Up Can Everything Get?

Merely comprehending any of the mammoth and mundane patterns which occupy our planet at the end of the twentieth century calls for diverse and exceptional skills. Relationships, desires, and obligations vary moment by moment. The value of goods, property, and the cost of borrowing change rapidly. Old rules no longer apply, but those who are able to see new designs linking the seemingly disconnected may be able to learn how something works. The order of things, such as it is, on the outside, might offer clues for making the world work better inside your head.

Juggling is a calisthenic for pattern seekers. A juggler combines imagination with sensitivity and concentration to work motion and smooth reciprocal change in his or her hands. It might be tantalizing to consider how similar creative focusing might add touches of balanced, constructive reason, and insight to fashionable thinking about global and everyday concerns, such as nuclear arms, money, the destruction of nature, or office buildings with windows that cannot be opened.

You Can Put It Together

At any level of juggling, there are always new patterns, routines, or skills that you might be able to add to what you know. You can try cascading mis-matched objects, tossing and interweaving two balls and a club, two rings and a ball, or two cups and a saucer, if you like. Make up your own odd variations, without missing a beat. You can work with one, or two, or ten partners, if you dare. The combinations are limitless.

You may be considering some of them. If you can juggle three, you have probably thought about four. If you can handle four, you might already be trying to juggle five in your head. (Hint: First roll balls out on the ground or up a slanted board, instead of trying to work out a complex pattern like a five-ball cascade in the air.)

For all the jugglers who speculate about such things, some have always come up with highly motivated ways to proceed. Now that you know something about juggling, see if the following archival jugglery gives you any special ideas.

Astonishing Acts

Albert Lucas, a performer with the *Ice Follies* show, juggles nine rings in a cascade while spinning one ring on his leg and balancing a ball on a mouthstick—while on ice skates. Albert cascaded five balls at age five and juggled on stage at the Tropicana Hotel in Las Vegas at age ten.

Anthony Gatto, age eight, in winning the 1981 Junior's Championship at the International Jugglers Association Convention, capped his performance by juggling four rings while spinning one on his leg, balancing a pole on his forehead and holding a ball on a mouthstick. Anthony can juggle six rings or balls, which is just a matter of juggling three rings in each hand, at the same time.

Lottie Brunn, ex–Ringling Brothers center ring star, "The Best Woman Juggler in the World," circa 1957, claims to be getting better after more than thirty years of juggling. Lottie juggled eight hoops at age fourteen.

The 1980 IJA Junior's title was won by Kaziah Tannenbaum, a young woman from Boulder, Colorado, who juggled clubs with greater skill and showmanship than seven male and two other female competitors.

Evgenij Biljauer performs for the Russian State Circus,

juggling five clubs overhand, under his legs and behind his back with two and three flips, or four clubs while bouncing a soccer ball on his head or balancing a fifth club on his noggin. He shares the current world record for cascading seven clubs with half a dozen other jugglers.

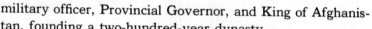

In 960 A.D., an Afghani slave named Alptegnin won his freedom by juggling atop a galloping horse, later became a military officer, Provincial Governor, and King of Afghanistan, founding a two-hundred-year dynasty.

Jean Claude, a Frenchman, juggles soccer balls, tapered cylinders and two dolls named Mick and Tony on his feet. He has worked half-time shows for the Harlem Globetrotters, played Las Vegas and appeared on the Merv Griffin TV show.

Larry Vaksman, "The Amazing Larry-V," from Philadelphia, Pennsylvania, won a juggling marathon at the Bergen Mall in Paramus, New Jersey by juggling three weighted tennis balls for two hours, fifty-four minutes, forty-six seconds without dropping. He averaged 146 throws per minute and handled more than 25,000 throws without a single miss. Larry is also able to control twelve objects in motion—by juggling three balls in one hand and a club and a basketball in the other, while spinning seven hula hoops around his waist.

Wolfe Bowart, a juggler with the Famous Bonzeralli Clowns, from Arizona, is able to juggle three balls for five minutes with his eyes closed.

In 1909, Paul Cinquevalli, an Italian juggler, was known for kicking up a sixty-pound cannon ball with his feet and catching it on the back of his neck in a reinforced-steel helmet.

Valeri Gurvey cascades three balls weighing twenty-six pounds each, as part of his act with the Moscow Circus.

Michael Lauziere juggled the entire twenty-six-plus mile course of the International Marathon of Montreal in 1981. His time was four hours, five minutes, and he made it the whole way without any drops.

In Whitewater, Wisconsin, Scott Damgaard ran a four-minute, thirty-seven-second mile while juggling three balls.

In the 1930s, Enrico Rastelli juggled six plates while spinning a ring and jumping rope. Still considered by many to be the greatest juggler ever—decades after his death—Rastelli holds world's records for juggling eight plates, and for juggling ten balls, which he did by juggling five in each hand.

The world's record for juggling objects is an eleven-hoop cascade thrown by Sergei Ignatov of the Moscow Circus. By now, Sergei may have stepped up to thirteen.

And irrepressible W. C. Fields, who once said he would prefer to be in Philadelphia, ended up, instead, on a United States postage stamp. Issued on the one-hundredth anniversary of the comedian's birth, January 29, 1980, the fifteen-cent stamp displays Fields juggling five balls.

Street Performing

You can still be noticed for your juggling—without ever accomplishing world record-breaking feats or lesser compulsions—right out in the street. Musicians, puppeteers, rope walkers, mimes, magicians, and jugglers play avenues and boulevards in San Francisco, New York, Boulder, Key West, Montreal, Boston, New Orleans, Rome, Paris, London, Canterbury, Dublin, Munich, Heidelberg, Vienna, and Athens. Any urban locale with decent foot traffic and amenable statutes could be your stage; student and tourist towns are especially recommended. You might find that old-fashioned street performing can be a satisfying accomplishment in and of itself. Giving cheer by enchanting passers-by is a delightful way to meet people and watch them greet each other. The audience is part of the act! And because your neighborhood, not some remote, invisible video empire, is the stage, street performing can involve direct human interchange, without the buffer of middling minds or technologies to dull its impact or deflect its potential.

If you can put together an engaging ten-minute-long routine (not as brief or easy as it may sound), you might even make some money by passing around your old top hat. Working and having fun at the same time might beat punching a time clock or your boss.

The Next Show

On an immediate level of what more you can do with juggling, the choices are fairly staggering. Taking the exercises this book covers, you may vary any pattern you know by throwing it narrower, wider, higher, lower, or in interwoven combinations that you juggle in time to your favorite music. You may juggle sitting down, lying on your back, or kneeling on the floor. Try getting down on your knees while juggling, and standing up without missing. Or bend far forward, and try juggling upside down, between your legs.

You might learn to throw from behind your back, under your legs, or over your shoulders, or you might want to try crossing your wrists in front of your waist—an excellent way to keep your hands down—to juggle.

You may learn to catch throws behind your back, under your legs, on the back of your neck, or in your mouth. Practice bouncing balls off each other in mid-air or off your head, if you like. Throw balls high in the sky and spin circles beneath them on roller skates until they come down, or try joggling for a new focus on your morning jog.

You might practice comedy juggling for laughs and teaching to keep your skills sharp. You might enjoy making your own props.

If you want to act showy, numbers juggling, club kick-ups, hat tricks, or juggling while riding a unicycle might be more your speed. You may learn to work with a diablo, cigar boxes, spinning plates, devil sticks, pogo sticks, tightrope, slackrope, stilts, or rolling globes for a hint of the refined balances jugglers can strive for.

Or you might learn to appreciate juggling as an art form, a means of self-expression that goes beyond flashy tricks and juggling for numbers. Because there are more possibilities for experimentation with fewer objects, you may find that you are utterly fascinated by controlling one ball; juggling it flawlessly calls for the grace and steadiness of a gymnast or a dancer. You might excel at juggling no balls at all.

Juggling is a tool that you can use forever.

Enjoy it.

JUST JUGGLE!

CHAPTER
16

Books, Props, and Groups

Books

There are other juggling books besides this one. Many are hard to find. This list can get you started on some valuable detective work.

Benge, Ken. *The Art of Juggling*. World Publications, 1977. 137 pages. Illustrated and photos. Basic instruction to advanced tricks, includes passing and sixty variations for handling three balls.

Burgess, Hovey. *Circus Techniques: Juggling Equilibristics Vaulting*. Drama Book Specialists, 1976. 162 pages. Photos.

Contains beginning, intermediate, and advanced skills in each area.

Carlo. *The Juggling Book*. Random House, 1974. 102 pages. Illustrated. Beginning to advanced tricks with balls, rings, clubs. A juggling textbook. One of the best books available; required reading for the serious juggling student.

Cassidy, John, and Rimbeaux, B. C. *Juggling for the Complete Klutz*. Klutz Enterprises, 1977. 29 pages. Illustrated. Amusing basic instructions, comes cleverly packaged with three bean bags.

Chamberlin, Rich. *Comedy Juggling,* 1981. 66 pages. Illustrated. Contains over 100 comedy ideas for jugglers, written by the current secretary/treasurer of the International Juggler's Association.

Cummins, Kent. *Bungling Juggling*. Elbee Company. 28 pages. Illustrated. Contains comedy ideas for jugglers.

DeMott, George. *Want to be a Juggler?* Montandon Magic. 81 pages. Illustrated. Basic ball instruction and instruction with many other props. Includes complete juggling and balancing routines; with 125 line drawings by the author.

Dittrich, Rudolf. *Juggling Made Easy*. Wilshire Book Company. 124 pages. Illustrated basic ball instruction and chapters on other props.

Humphrey, Ron. *Juggling for Fun and Entertainment*. Charles Tuttle Company. Includes basic juggling instruction; has chapter on fire juggling.

Joy of Juggling. Juggle Bug, 1979. 43 pages. Illustrated. Basic ball juggling with some advanced tricks.

Meyer, Charles. *How to be a Juggler*. David McKay Company. 56 pages. Photos. Basic juggling instruction.

Sikorsky, Thomas. *Juggling: the Possible Dream*. 52 pages. Illustrated. Basic instruction with some advanced tricks.

Silverberg, Robert. *Lord Valentine's Castle*. Bantam Science Fiction, 1981. 447 pages. A novel about an epic quest by a band of human and extraterrestrial jugglers on a giant, distant planet many thousands of years from now. Delightful reading spiced by incisive, knowledgeable juggling information. Highly recommended.

Stubblefield, W. C. *Clown Magic, Juggling, Sight Bits*. 1969. 62 pages. Photos and illustrations. Comedy ideas for jugglers based on performer Stubby the Clown's fifty years of clowning, juggling, and performing magic.

Zeithen, Karl-Heinz. *4,000 Years of Juggling Volume I*. Michel Poignant, Sainte Genevieve, France, 1980. Photos, facts, juggling history. 290 photographs depicting skill, diversity, and artistry of juggling from the first paintings of jugglers on the wall of an Egyptian tomb dating from 4600 B.C. to the twentieth century. An astounding reference work. Cost, $100. Volume II soon to be available.

Many of these books may be found in libraries. Some are sold by propmakers, in magic shops, novelty shops, or are available directly from the publishers. As juggling gains in popularity, more titles are turning up in bookstores.

Propmakers

Professional juggling props are about as easy to find as juggling books. Someday all these things will be more accessible. For now, many magic and novelty shops carry stock.

Most propmakers will send you a catalog and a price sheet for a stamped return envelope.

The Alit Ohba Circus: 1848 Fell Street, San Francisco, CA 94117. (415) 386-5208. Cigar boxes.

Kent Bagnall: 1337 Trelane Avenue, Crestwood, MO 63126. (314) 961-2189. Cigar boxes.

Chameleon Cubes: 934 Spruce, Boulder, CO 80302. Juggling cubes.

Creative Hand: Box 434, Greenbelt, MD 20770. (301) 471-6350. Beanbags with drawstring sack.

Ben Decker—The Prop Shop: 4025 John Street, San Diego, CA 92106. Cigar boxes; rings.

Brian Dube: 25 Park Place, second floor, New York, NY 10007. (212) 619-2182. Clubs; rings; torches; devil sticks; diablos; cigar boxes; balls; rola-bolas.

Juggle Bug, Inc.: 23004 107th Place West, Edmonds, WA 98020. (206) 542-2030. Rings; clubs; balls; cigar boxes; scarves; diablos; devil sticks; hats.

The Juggling Arts: 612 Calpella Drive, San Jose, CA 95136. (408) 267-8237. Clubs; spinning plate and dowels; spinning bowl and dowels; mouth pieces; devil sticks; balls.

Pat: Box 412, Mendocino, CA 95460. Juggling bags.

Stuart Raynolds: 2716 Silverside Road, Wilmington, DE 19810. Clubs; cigar boxes; foot juggling balls; hoops; plates.

TAL Worldwide Productions, Inc: P.O. Box 3906, Baltimore, MD 21222. Juggling axes; clown props; catalog $2.00.

Todd Smith Juggling Props: 1624 Compton, Cleveland, OH 44118. (216) 432-6358. Clubs; rings; cigar boxes; bean bags; balls.

Zen Products: 1715 Waller Street, San Francisco, CA 94117. Juggling bags; clubs; torches.

Groups

There are juggling groups all over the planet, from the International Jugglers Association, with several thousand members, to smaller local organizations. Affiliation is generally informal, inexpensive (or free!), and may be a good way to locate props and books, learn new tricks, and meet juggling partners and friends.

The International Jugglers Association is the largest juggler's group worldwide. Founded in 1947 by twelve jugglers who wanted to save what they thought was a dying art, the organization exists to promote juggling and assist jugglers. Today the IJA holds yearly conventions where pro and amateur jugglers meet to show off, swap tricks, hold workshops, and compete for world championships. Jugglers from the United States, Canada, and Europe registered for the Cleveland convention in 1981, breaking attendance records for the sixth year in a row.

The IJA is the certifying authority for juggling records recognized by World Almanacs and *The Guinness Book of World Records*. Yearly dues of thirteen dollars covers a one-year subscription to the IJA's *Jugglers World* magazine, which may be the best currently updated source of state-of-the-art juggling information available. Contact: IJA, P.O. Box 29, Kenmore, NY 14217.

Local juggling groups:

Akron, OH—Rubber City Jugglers meet Tuesdays. Kevin Delrange at (216) 724-0649.

Anchorage, AK—Juggling class meets Wednesday, 7–9 P.M.

Anchorage Community College multipurpose room. Call Jim Kerr at (907) 278-4621.

Atlanta, GA—Atlanta Jugglers Association meets Tuesday and Thursday, 6– 8 P.M., Moreland School, corner of Euclid and Austin Avenues NE. Call Toni Shifalo at (404) 373-7175.

Baltimore, MD—The Baltimore Jugglers Association meets Monday from 6:30– 10 P.M. in the Wyman Park Multi-Purpose Center, 501 W. 30th Street. Call Janet Sanford at (301) 323-6613.

Binghamton, NY—The Binghamton Juggling Institute meets at SUNY, Binghamton, U.U. 221, Thursday, 7– 10 P.M. Call Bruce Eisendorf at (607) 770-8052.

Boulder, CO—The Boulder Juggling Club meets daily from 10 A.M.– 6 P.M in the Balch Fieldhouse. Auditions held the first Thursday of every month. Write the Boulder Juggling Club, 1802 Walnut, Boulder, CO 80302.

Boston, MA—The MIT Juggle Club meets Sundays, from 1:30– 5:30 P.M. in the lobby of Building 13 on campus. Warm days, the meeting will be in front of the student center. Call Arthur Lewbel at (617) 628-3702.

Buffalo, NY—The Buffalo Juggling Club meets regularly. Call Rich Chamberlin at (716) 873-8193.

Burlington, VT—Jugglers meet in Battery Park Mondays, from 5:30– 8 P.M. Call Henry Lappen at (802) 658-3757 or 658-5939.

Cambridge, England—Jugglers meet Tuesday, 8– 10 P.M. in the Kennedy Room, Cambridge Union, Roundchurch Street. Contact Adam Wein (Churchill College) or Claudia Kennedy (Queens' College).

Charlotte, NC—The Charlotte Jugglers Association meets Tuesday, 7– 9 P.M. in Spirit Square. Call Pat Cox at (704) 376-7798.

Charlottesville, VA—The Apples and Bananas Juggling Club meets throughout the year. Call Michael Parent at (703) 296-7011 or Larry Goldstein at 979-7720.

Chicago, IL—The Chicago Society of Juggling meets at Triton Junior College, 2000 5th Avenue, River Grove on Thursday from 7:30 P.M. until. Call Mike Vondruska at (312) 766-2298.

Cleveland, OH—The Case Western Reserve University club meets Wednesday at 5 P.M. in Thwing Center.

Columbia, MO—The Y's Jugglers meet Sunday, 1–4 P.M. on the practice field at the Hearnes Multi-purpose Building. Tuesdays from 6–9 P.M. in rooms 208/210 of the Brady Commons of the University of Missouri campus.

Copenhagen, Denmark—Jugglers meet Tuesday, 5–7 P.M. in the Judo Room of Svanemollehallen. Call Jens Brix Christiansen at 01-295800 or 02-441113.

Davidson, NC—Jugglers meet Monday, 7–9 P.M. in the College Union. Call Bill Giduz at (704) 892-1296 or 892-2000.

Dubuque, IA—University of Iowa Juggling Club meets Sunday at 2 P.M., Thursday at 3 P.M., at the U. of I. fieldhouse. Call Gary Podolsky at (319) 337-6957, or Randy Shukar at 338-5137.

Duluth, MN—The Dawn to Dusk Juggling Club meets weekdays in the basement of the State Employment Service Building. Call Larry Ketola at (218) 724-2774.

Durham, NH—The U.N.H. Club meets Wednesday 7–11 P.M in the Memorial Union Building on campus. Call Mark Neisser at (603) 749-2798.

East Lansing, MI—The M.S.U. jugglers meet Tuesday from 6–8:30 P.M. at the Union Tower Room. Call Daniel Sadoff at (517) 623-6012.

Erie, PA—Jugglers meet Tuesday, 6:30–9:30 P.M. in the YWCA at 130 W. 8th Street. Call Bill Dietrich at (814) 825-7369.

Eugene, OR—Classes are held Monday and Tuesday nights at the Lane Community College. Call Tom Dewart at (503) 683-8344 or Janet Planet 683-8956.

Evanston, IL—Jugglers meet Wednesday, 8 P.M. at the Robert Crown Center, 801 Main Street. Call Jack Snarr at (312) 869-4606.

Fort Wayne, IN—Jugglers Anonymous meets Saturday noon–2 P.M. at Franke Park, near the zoo. Call Charlie Willer at (219) 426-8998 or Larry Thompson at 483-6026.

Gardena, CA—Jugglers meet Wednesday from 7–10 P.M. in Freeman Park. Call Andy Lintz at (213) 316-1702.

Geneva, NY—The Finger Lakes Juggling Club meets at the Salvation Army Building every third Thursday, at 7 P.M. Call Rich Stewart at (315) 536-0579.

Hermosa Beach, CA—South Bay jugglers meet Wednesday and Sunday, 1 P.M. till dark. Hermosa Pier. Andy Lintz at (213) 316-1702.

Hookset, NH—The New Hampshire Juggling Club meets Monday 8 P.M. at the Gyminney Cricket School of Gymnastics, Mount St. Mary's, Route 3. Call (603) 749-2798.

Houston, TX—The Houston Jugglers Association meets Sunday, 3:30 P.M. at Bell Park, on Montrose Avenue at Milford Street. Call Jay Herson at (713) 661-8327.

Johnstown, PA—For juggling information, call Dick Lorditch at (814) 536-0579.

Lexington, KY—Jugglers meet Monday 7:30–9 P.M. at Woodland Park. Call Steven Roenker or Jean St. John at (606) 231-0565.

Lincoln, NE—The Lincoln Jugglers meet Sunday at Cooper Park, 8th and D Street. Call Jim or Dennis at (402) 474-4800.

London, England—Tim Batson's Juggling Workshop is held at the Pineapple Dance Center, 7 Langley Street, London WC2, on Sunday afternoons.

Madison, WI—Jugglers meet Sunday at 2 P.M. at Union South on the corner of Randall and Dayton Street. Just whistle!

Minneapolis, MN—Jugglers meet Wednesday, 5:30 P.M. to dark at Matthews Center, two blocks south of 28th and E. Franklin. Call John Linn at (612) 788-0342.

Minneapolis, MN—The University of Minnesota Juggling Club meets Monday and Thursday 4–6 P.M. in Norris Gym #60. An informal gathering is held Mondays in the winter, 6–9 P.M. at Seward School, 2309 28th Avenue South. Call Dan Westacott at (612) 788-5807.

New York, NY—The Brian Dube Studios offer free juggling from 4–6 P.M. Thursday, noon–2 P.M. Friday, at 25 Park Place. Call Brian Dube at (212) 619-2182.

New York, NY—The Flying Debris Juggling Club meets Sunday afternoons in Central Park at 77th Street. Go down the path at the end of the stone wall on the left. Call Steve Schneider at (212) 666-2224.

North Hollywood, CA—Jugglers meet at L.A. Valley College Thursday, 8:30 P.M. Call Bob Steurer at (213) 448-0382.

Northridge, CA—California State University at Northridge offers juggling and propmaking classes Monday and Wednesday from 6:30–8:30 P.M. Call John Spurny at (213) 907-1877.

Pasadena, CA—Jugglers meet Saturday, 9 A.M. 'til noon at Hamilton Elementary School. Call Hal Gordon at (213) 352-6182.

Plymouth, IN—The Notre Dame Juggling Club meets Thursday, 7–9 P.M. in the ballroom above the Huddle in the Fortune Building. Call Al Eisenhour at (219) 936-8564 or Bob Rice 674-8074.

Portland, OR—Jugglers meet at Reed College Wednesday, 7–9 P.M. in the gym. Call Joe Buhler at (503) 775-9095.

Redding, CA—Jugglers meet Tuesday and Thursday at Shasta College. Contact John Kelly at 237 Boulder Cr. #D, Redding, CA 96003.

Rochester, NY—The Rochester Juggling Club meets occasionally. Call Greg Moss at (716) 671-1143.

St. Cloud, MN—St. Cloud State University juggling club meets Wednesday 12–1 P.M. in Eastman Gym. Call Phil Moen at (612) 633-2390.

St. Louis, MO—Jugglers meet Friday at 7 P.M. at the Mid-County Library and Sunday at 1 P.M. at Shaw Park. Call Kent Bagnall at (314) 961-2819.

San Diego, CA—The U.C.S.D. Juggling Club meets Wednesday from noon to 3 P.M. on the Muir Lawn. Call Ben Decker at (714) 222-0100.

San Francisco, CA—Jugglers meet all day Sunday in Golden Gate Park near the Conservatory.

San Luis Obisbo, CA—Jugglers meet Sunday, 1–4 P.M. in Mitchell Park. Call Mary Siefert at (805) 541-3506.

Santa Barbara, CA—UCSB classes meet occasionally. Call Rebecca Norris at (805) 961-3738 daytime.

Seattle, WA—Jugglers meet at the Seattle Center House, 3–5 P.M., Saturday. Contact Juggler's Hotline (206) 542-2030.

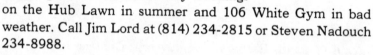

State College, PA—The Penn State Juggling Club meets Monday evenings on the Hub Lawn in summer and 106 White Gym in bad weather. Call Jim Lord at (814) 234-2815 or Steven Nadouch 234-8988.

Sunnyvale, CA—Jugglers meet at Sunnyvale Community Center Saturday noon—4 P.M. Call Barry Bakalor at (408) 247-3123.

Tampa Bay, FL—Jugglers meet Thursday 6–9 P.M. Call Ed Kosco (813) 527-1716.

Van Nuys, CA—The L.A. Valley College Juggling Forum meets Thursday, 8–10:30 P.M. in the gym. Call Keith Emery at (213) 360-9200.

Tokyo, Japan—Meetings on Sunday at 2 P.M., at NHK Plaza, near Meiji Jingu Park. Call Jack Plimpton at 03-463-8231.

Washington, DC—Jugglers meet Friday, 6–9 P.M. at the Chevy Chase Community Center, Connecticut and McKinley Avenue, NW. Call Shelly Harris at (202) 667-5307.

Other gatherings for jugglers:

Atlanta Groundhog Day Jugglers Festival—an annual February affair. Contact Atlanta Jugglers Association for information.

European IJA Convention—held in September. 1982's was in Copenhagen, Denmark, attended by jugglers from Australia, Denmark, England, France, Holland, India, Italy, Scotland, Switzerland, United States, and West Germany. Contact IJA-USA for information.

International Jugglers Association Convention—held in July. 1982's was in Santa Barbara, CA. This is the largest yearly gathering of jugglers in the world. Features festivities, events, and workshops. Contact IJA, Box 29, Kenmore, NY 14217, for more information.

Isla Vista Jugglers Festival—an informal gathering held north of Santa Barbara, CA in April. Contact John Zuber, 6831 Fortuna Rd., Isla Vista, CA 93117, (805) 685-5945, for information.

Jugglefest—held in April in Columbia, MO, features a public show and endurance competition. Contact Bruce Hinterleitner, 114 Gentry Hall, Columbia, MO 65211, (314) 449-5768, for information.

Midwest Jugglers Convention—held in June at the University of Iowa, Iowa City, IA. Events include juggling races, numbers competitions, workshops, a party and a public show. Prizes are awarded. Contact Jim Calkins, U of I Jugglers, Box 813 Dept. C, Iowa City, IA 52244, (319) 337-3480, for information.

Return to Amherst Spring Mini-Convention—held in April at the Robert Crown Center at Hampshire College, site of the 1979 IJA Convention. Festivities include workshops, a public show, and open juggling. Contact Eric Roberts, 668A Washington St. #7, Wellesley, MA 02181, (617) 237-9485, for information.

Rochester Institute of Technology Spring Juggle-In—held in May. Contact Greg Moss, 479 Mansey Lane, Rochester, NY 14625, (716) 671-1143, for information.

San Francisco County Fair—held in early summer, features contests for jugglers, including five-ball endurance juggling, three-eggs juggling with mandatory tricks and three-object variety juggling judged according to how difficult chosen objects are to juggle. New props are awarded as prizes. Contact Michael Rega (c/o Nelson), 210 Clayton St., San Francisco, CA 94117, (415) 668-4605, for information.

St. Fred's Day Jugglers Invitational—held in April in Ft. Wayne, IN. Events include obstacle course juggling, team egg juggling, marathon contests, joggling, the world's largest team juggle, and free juggling lessons. Contact Charlie Willer, Jugglers Anonymous, 107 S. Clinton, Ft. Wayne, IN 46802, (219) 426-8988 or 483-6026, for information.

Occasional shopping center promotions and charity fund-raising events feature juggling marathons where all you need to do to enter is a three-ball cascade. Some contests offer props as prizes, or money! If your area has none scheduled, organize your own event. Juggling is taking hold; let yourself go.

Catalog

If you are interested in a list of fine Paperback
books, covering a wide range of subjects
and interests, send your name and address,
requesting your free catalog, to:

McGraw-Hill Paperbacks
1221 Avenue of Americas
New York, N.Y. 10020

Steve Cohen

JUST JUGGLE

JUST JUGGLE details an easy method b
which anyone can learn to juggle.

Writing with knowledge and good humo
the author divides juggling into componen
parts by explaining what to juggle, how to
stand, where to practice, with sections on
using hands, rhythm, reflexes. Illustration
trajectory diagrams, and an animated flip
sequence supplement the text.

Besides dealing with the exercise and
entertainment values of juggling, the auth
explores its meditative and relaxation potentials. Juggling, he feels, meshes right
brain/left brain functions to promote over-
all body and mind balance and provides a
satisfying, noncompetitive way to relax.

"Efficient juggling takes physical skill,
agility, dexterity," writes Cohen. "It wastes
no motion, moves quickly outside consciou
thought, becomes instinctual dance, freein
the mind to ponder, to learn to stretch beyond known limits of strength and power, t
become more aware. Juggling compresses
energy into a concentrated way of looking,
of feeling, of seeing that there is always a
cohesive flow, no matter how chaotic thing
may appear to be. And remember that juggling is fun, too, maybe even silly, but you
earn your good time with skillful concentration, coordination, control, and
imagination."

Steve Cohen is a novelist, travel editor,
and has taught juggling for five years.

 McGraw Hill

ISBN 0-07-011623-7